Steps to God's Presence

Dag Heward-Mills

Parchment House

Unless otherwise stated, all Scripture quotations are taken from the King James Version of the Bible.

STEPS TO GOD'S PRESENCE

First published 2019 by Parchment House
1st Printing 2019

Find out more about Dag Heward-Mills at:

Healing Jesus Campaign
Email: evangelist@daghewardmills.org
Website: www.daghewardmills.org
Facebook: Dag Heward-Mills
Twitter: @EvangelistDag

ISBN: 978-1-64329-195-6

Contents

CHAPTER 1

Where Has the Presence of God Been?

And they heard the voice of the Lord God walking in the garden in the cool of the day: and ADAM AND HIS WIFE HID THEMSELVES FROM THE PRESENCE OF THE LORD GOD amongst the trees of the garden. And the Lord God called unto Adam, and said unto him, where art thou?

Genesis 3:8-9

1. **The presence of God was with Adam. Everyday, the Lord God would fellowship with Adam and Eve in the cool of the day.**

And they heard the voice of the Lord God walking in the garden in the cool of the day: and ADAM AND HIS WIFE HID THEMSELVES FROM THE PRESENCE OF THE LORD GOD amongst the trees of the garden. And the Lord God called unto Adam, and said unto him, where art thou?

Genesis 3:8-9

2. **The presence of God was with Enoch.**

ENOCH WALKED WITH GOD after he fathered Methuselah 300 years and had other sons and daughters.

Genesis 5:22 (ESV)

3. **The presence of God was with Abraham.**

Then THE LORD APPEARED TO ABRAM and said, "To your offspring I will give this land." So he us built there an altar to the Lord, who had appeared to him.

Genesis 12:7 (ESV)

4. **The presence of God was with Isaac.**

And the Lord appeared unto him the same night, and said, I am the God of Abraham thy father: fear not, FOR I AM WITH THEE, and will bless thee, and multiply thy seed for my servant Abraham's sake.

Genesis 26:24

5. **The presence of God was with Jacob.**

BEHOLD, I AM WITH YOU and will keep you wherever you go, and will bring you back to this land. For I will not leave you until I have done what I have promised you." Then Jacob awoke from his sleep and said, "Surely the Lord is in this place, and I did not know it."

And he was afraid and said, "How awesome is this place! This is none other than the house of God, and this is the gate of heaven."

Genesis 28:15-17 (ESV)

6. The presence of God was with Joseph.

THE LORD WAS WITH JOSEPH, and he became a successful man, and he was in the house of his Egyptian master.

Genesis 39:2 (ESV)

7. The presence of God was with Moses.

Just as we obeyed Moses in all things, so we will obey you. Only may the Lord your God be with you, as he was with Moses!

Joshua 1:17 (ESV)

8. The presence of God was found in the Tabernacle built by Moses.

There I will meet with you, and from above the mercy seat, from between the two cherubim that are on the ark of the testimony, I will speak with you about all that I will give you in commandment for the people of Israel.

Exodus 25:22 (ESV)

The Tabernacle has had different names at different times. The Tabernacle has been called the Tabernacle of the Congregation, the Tabernacle of Witness, the Tent of Witness, the Tabernacle of Moses, the Wilderness Tabernacle.

The Tabernacle came into existence about a year after the children of Israel crossed the Red Sea. The Tabernacle existed for four hundred years, until King Solomon built the first temple in Jerusalem.

The Tabernacle was always situated in the very centre of the camp of the Israelites. The Tabernacle took seven months to build. When it was finished, a cloud and a pillar of fire descended on it, representing the presence of God.

The details for the construction of the Tabernacle were received by Moses on Mount Sinai. The cost of building the Tabernacle was borne by the children of Israel who had come out of Egypt with much wealth.

> Take ye from among you an offering unto the Lord: whosoever is of a willing heart, let him bring it, an offering of the Lord; gold, and silver, and brass, And blue, and purple, and scarlet, and fine linen, and goats' hair, And rams' skins dyed red, and badgers' skins, and shittim wood, And oil for the light, and spices for anointing oil, and for the sweet incense, And onyx stones, and stones to be set for the ephod, and for the breastplate. And every wise hearted among you shall come, and make all that the Lord hath commanded; The Tabernacle, his tent, and his covering, his taches, and his boards, his bars, his pillars, and his sockets,
>
> Exodus 35:5-11

The Tabernacle was moved many times. Every time the Israelites moved, the whole Tabernacle was packed into carts and carried by the Israelites. The Ark of the Covenant was always carried by the Levites themselves.

9. The Tabernacle, about thirty-eight years, was moved to Kadesh-barnea.

> And the time from our leaving Kadesh-barnea until we crossed the brook Zered was thirty-eight years, until the entire generation, that is, the men of war, had perished from the camp, as the Lord had sworn to them.
>
> Deuteronomy 2:14 (ESV)

10. The Tabernacle crossed the River Jordan into The Promised Land.

And Joshua said to the priests, "Take up the Ark of the Covenant and pass on before the people." So they took up the Ark of the Covenant and went before the people. The Lord said to Joshua, "Today I will begin to exalt you in the sight of all Israel, that they may know that, as I was with Moses, so I will be with you.

Joshua 3:6-7 (ESV)

11. The next home of the Tabernacle was Shiloh, where it remained till the time of the judges.

And when the people were come into the camp, the elders of Israel said, Wherefore hath the Lord smitten us to day before the Philistines? Let us fetch the ark of the covenant of the Lord out of Shiloh unto us, that, when it cometh among us, it may save us out of the hand of our enemies. SO THE PEOPLE SENT TO SHILOH, THAT THEY MIGHT BRING FROM THENCE THE ARK OF THE COVENANT OF THE LORD OF HOSTS, which dwelleth between the cherubims: and the two sons of Eli, Hophni and Phinehas, were there with the ark of the covenant of God.

1 Samuel 4:3-4

12. The Ark of the Covenant which was kept in the Tabernacle was captured by the Philistines and brought to Ashdod.

And the Philistines took the ark of God, and brought it from Ebenezer unto ASHDOD.

1 Samuel 5:1

13. The next home for the Tabernacle was Gath.

They sent therefore and gathered all the lords of the Philistines unto them, and said, What shall we do with the ark of the God of Israel? And they answered, let the ark of the God of Israel be carried about unto GATH. And they carried the ark of the God of Israel about thither.

1 Samuel 5:8

14. The next home of the Tabernacle was Ekron.

So they sent the ark of God to EKRON. But as soon as the ark of God came to Ekron, the people of Ekron cried out, "They have brought around to us the ark of the God of Israel to kill us and our people."

1 Samuel 5:10 (ESV)

15. The next home of the Tabernacle was Beth-shemesh.

And take the ark of the Lord and place it on the cart and put in a box at its side the figures of gold, which you are returning to him as a guilt offering. Then send it off and let it go its way and watch. If it goes up on the way to its own land, to BETH-SHEMESH, then it is he who has done us this great harm, but if not, then we shall know that it is not his hand that struck us; it happened to us by coincidence....

Now the people of BETH-SHEMESH were reaping their wheat harvest in the valley. And when they lifted up their eyes and saw the ark, they rejoiced to see it. The cart came into the field of Joshua of BETH-SHEMESH and stopped there. A great stone was there. And they split up the wood of the cart and offered the cows as a burnt offering to the Lord. And the Levites took down the ark of the Lord and the box that was beside it, in which were the golden figures, and set them upon the great stone. And the men of BETH-SHEMESH offered burnt offerings and sacrificed sacrifices on that day to the Lord.

1 Samuel 6:8-9, 13-15 (ESV)

16. The next home of the Tabernacle was Kiriathjearim.

And the men of KIRJATHJEARIM came, and fetched up the ark of the Lord, and brought it into the house of Abinadab in the hill, and sanctified Eleazar his son to keep the ark of the Lord. And it came to pass, while the ark abode in Kirjathjearim, that the time was long; for it was twenty years: and all the house of Israel lamented after the Lord.

1 Samuel 7:1-2

17. The next home of the Tabernacle was Jerusalem. King David had the ark brought to Jerusalem from the house of Abinadab in Gibeah.

And they brought it out of the house of Abinadab which was at Gibeah, accompanying the ark of God: and Ahio went before the ark. And David and all the house of Israel played before the Lord on all manner of instruments made of fir wood, even on harps, and on psalteries, and on timbrels, and on cornets, and on cymbals.

2 Samuel 6:4-5

So David and all the house of Israel brought up the ark of the Lord with shouting, and with the sound of the trumpet. And AS THE ARK OF THE LORD CAME INTO THE CITY OF DAVID, Michal Saul's daughter looked through a window, and saw king David leaping and dancing before the Lord; and she despised him in her heart.

2 Samuel 6:15-16

18. The temple was built by Solomon and the presence of God was found in the temple from then on.

Then said Solomon, The Lord hath said that he would dwell in the thick darkness. But I HAVE BUILT AN HOUSE OF HABITATION FOR THEE, AND A PLACE FOR THY DWELLING FOR EVER. And the king turned his face, and blessed the whole congregation of Israel: and all the congregation of Israel stood. And he said, Blessed be the Lord God of Israel, who hath with his hands fulfilled that which he spake with his mouth to my father David, saying, Since the day that I brought forth my people out of the land of Egypt I chose no city among all the tribes of Israel to build an house in, that my name might be there; neither chose I any man to be a ruler over my people Israel: But I have chosen Jerusalem, that my name might be there; and have chosen David to be over my people Israel. Now it was in the heart of David my father to build an house for the name of the Lord God of Israel.

2 Chronicles 6:1-7

19. When Jesus died, the veil in the temple was torn and the presence of God moved out from the temple.

And the veil of the temple was rent in twain from the top to the bottom.

Mark 15:38

20. You are now the temple of God.

And what agreement hath the temple of God with idols? FOR YE ARE THE TEMPLE OF THE LIVING GOD; AS GOD HATH SAID, I WILL DWELL IN THEM, and walk in them; and I will be their God, and they shall be my people.

2 Corinthians 6:16

CHAPTER 2

The Mystery of God's Residence

It was therefore necessary that the PATTERNS OF THINGS IN THE HEAVENS should be purified with these; but the heavenly things themselves with better sacrifices than these. For Christ is not entered into the holy places made with hands, which are the FIGURES OF THE TRUE; but into heaven itself, now to appear in the presence of God for us:

Hebrews 9:23-24

God's mysterious residence is called the Tabernacle. In the Old Testament, God instructed His people to create an environment where His presence would dwell. Even you, cannot live or exist in every environment. How much more Almighty God? God's presence cannot flourish everywhere. There are certain things that are contrary to His presence. He will simply not stay everywhere. The key to the presence of God is found in the Old Testament. The way to get into the presence of God is described vividly in the Old Testament.

The Tabernacle was a carefully constructed mysterious residence where the presence of God was to be manifested. Great care was given to detail in the construction of this special "God environment". The building of the Tabernacle will always be a key to understanding the presence of God. Different Hebrew words are translated into the word "Tabernacle".

The word "Tabernacle" is translated from the word "Mishkan" and it means "residence". God's mysterious residence was constructed by the Israelites. Mishkan (God's residence) is a place where God settles, abides and resides. Your residence is where you settle, abide and reside. God's residence is where He settles and dwells comfortably. The Tabernacle was the place where God's mysterious presence dwelt. Everywhere you see the word "Tabernacle", simply replace it with the words "God's residence".

> **According to all that I shew thee, after the pattern of the Tabernacle (*Residence)*, and the pattern of all the instruments thereof, even so shall ye make it.**
>
> **Exodus 25:9**

The word "Sanctuary" is translated from the word "Miqdash" and it means "Holy Place" or "Sanctuary". God's instruction was, "Build me a holy and hallowed place where I can reside."

> **And let them make me a sanctuary (*Holy Place*); that I may dwell among them.**
>
> **Exodus 25:8**

I once came to a town on one of my journeys, where I simply could not find any place with a good enough environment for me to stay in. I simply decided to stay in the car since that was a more conducive environment for me. That village did not have any room where I could lay my head. The crusade car was the best environment for me. I could understand how God would not come into certain places. If indeed we want God to dwell in our midst, it is important for us to study the instructions He gave for the building of a place that can hold His presence. We can glean some valuable information about what God likes and what He does not like. We must learn about what God is comfortable with and what He simply does not want. The Tabernacle (God's Residence) is the structure which God instructed to be built to contain His presence.

Seven Things You Should Know about God's Residence

1. God wants His presence to dwell in the midst of His people.

Prophetically, God has always decided to dwell in the midst of His people. Since that is the will of God, it is important for us to desire to have God residing in our midst. We must work to have God dwelling in our midst.

> Sing and rejoice, O daughter of Zion: for, lo, I come, and I WILL DWELL IN THE MIDST OF THEE, saith the Lord. And MANY NATIONS SHALL BE JOINED to the Lord in that day, and shall be my people: and I WILL DWELL IN THE MIDST OF THEE, and thou shalt know that the Lord of hosts hath sent me unto thee.
>
> And the Lord shall inherit Judah his portion in the holy land, and shall choose Jerusalem again. Be silent, O all flesh, before the Lord: for he is raised up out of his holy habitation.
>
> Zechariah 2:10-13

2. The Tabernacle is an environment that God's presence can dwell in.

God directed Moses to create an environment where His presence could dwell and exist amongst us. This environment that Moses was asked to create was called the Tabernacle. It is therefore important to us to learn about the environment that *God defined and described* as a residence for Himself. God knows exactly what He can dwell in. Another name you could give the Tabernacle is "*God's environment.*"

> And the Lord spake unto Moses, saying, Speak unto the children of Israel, that they bring me an offering: of every man that giveth it willingly with his heart ye shall take my offering.
>
> And this is the offering which ye shall take of them; gold, and silver, and brass, And blue, and purple, and scarlet, and fine linen, and goats 'hair, And rams' skins dyed red, and badgers 'skins, and shittim wood, Oil for the light, spices for anointing oil, and for sweet incense, Onyx stones, and stones to be set in the ephod, and in the breastplate.
>
> And LET THEM MAKE ME A SANCTUARY; THAT I MAY DWELL AMONG THEM. ACCORDING TO ALL THAT I SHEW THEE, AFTER THE PATTERN OF THE TABERNACLE, AND THE PATTERN OF ALL THE INSTRUMENTS THEREOF, EVEN SO SHALL YE MAKE IT.
>
> Exodus 25:1-9

3. The earthly Tabernacle is only a version of God's heavenly residence.

Christ showed us the way to the everlasting presence of God. Almighty God lives in a Tabernacle not made with hands. Christ came to show us how we can access that Tabernacle not made with hands. In Christ, we learn that Moses' Tabernacle was just a figure of what is in Heaven.

Now when these things were thus ordained, the priests went always into the first Tabernacle, accomplishing the service of God.

But into the second went the high priest alone once every year, not without blood, which he offered for himself, and for the errors of the people: the Holy Ghost this signifying, that the way into the holiest of all was not yet made manifest, while as the first Tabernacle was yet standing: Which was a figure for the time then present, in which were offered both gifts and sacrifices, that could not make him that did the service perfect, as pertaining to the conscience; which stood only in meats and drinks, and divers washings, and carnal ordinances, imposed on them until the time of reformation.

BUT CHRIST BEING COME AN HIGH PRIEST OF GOOD THINGS TO COME, BY A GREATER AND MORE PERFECT TABERNACLE, NOT MADE WITH HANDS, that is to say, not of this building;

Hebrews 9:6-11

4. The earthly tabernacle is a pattern for God's heavenly residence.

The tabernacle will forever be a figurative guide on the way into the presence of God. Patterns that God loves are revealed in the Tabernacle. Always remember that the Tabernacle is an environment in which God can dwell.

It was therefore necessary that the PATTERNS OF THINGS IN THE HEAVENS should be purified with these; but the heavenly things themselves with better sacrifices than these. For Christ is not entered into the holy places made with hands, which are the FIGURES OF THE TRUE; but into heaven itself, now to appear in the presence of God for us:

Hebrews 9:23-24

5. The many details of God's residence are important to understand God's residence.

> Then verily the first covenant had also ordinances of divine service, and a worldly sanctuary. For there was a Tabernacle made; the first, wherein was the candlestick, and the table, and the shewbread; which is called the sanctuary. And after the second veil, the Tabernacle which is called the Holiest of all; Which had the golden censer, and the ark of the covenant overlaid round about with gold, wherein was the golden pot that had manna, and Aaron's rod that budded, and the tables of the covenant; And over it the cherubims of glory shadowing the mercyseat; of which we cannot now speak particularly.
>
> Hebrews 9:1-5

There are no meaningless details in the Bible. Every detail of the Tabernacle is a revelation of something important about God's residence.

To take some of these details for granted is to make a big mistake. Little things often make a big difference. In relating to important people, it is important to take their little things seriously. You can lose favour with an important person when you take the little things he likes for granted. Never trivialise an instruction or a detail given to you by an important person. After all, a little detail to an important person must be a very big thing because he is an important person.

6. At the cross, the veil was torn so we could experience the presence of God forever.

> Jesus, when he had cried again with a loud voice, yielded up the ghost. And, behold, the veil of the temple was rent in twain from the top to the bottom; and the earth did quake, and the rocks rent;
>
> Matthew 27:50-51

Prophetically, when Jesus died on the cross, the veil that separated man from God was broken. This signified that a new and closer relationship between God and man was now possible. It is time for us to seek a closer relationship with God. It is time for us to seek to create an environment in which God can dwell. The environment in which God can dwell is called the Tabernacle.

7. The presence of God is necessary for us.

> IT WAS THEREFORE NECESSARY that the patterns of things in the heavens should be purified with these; but the heavenly things themselves with better sacrifices than these. For Christ is not entered into the holy places made with hands, which are the figures of the true; but into heaven itself, now to appear in the presence of God FOR US:
>
> Hebrews 9:23-24

It is necessary that the pattern of things in heaven should be revealed on earth. There are so many benefits for having the presence of God in our lives. Protection, health, guidance and prosperity are all benefits of the presence of God. Through your study of the details of the Tabernacle, you will come to know wonderful revelations that are very important in order to have the presence of God always in your life and ministry.

I believe you are desirous of the presence of God. Through this book, God's presence will be manifested in your life and ministry.

CHAPTER 3

A Tour of God's Residence

In Judah is God known: his name is great in Israel. In Salem also is HIS TABERNACLE, AND HIS DWELLING PLACE in Zion.

Psalms 76:1-2

The best picture of God's residence is the Tabernacle. By understanding the design, the layout, the arrangement of items, the furniture, the colours as well as other minute details of God's residence, you will understand how to navigate in the presence of God. Let us now have a quick overview of what the Tabernacle looked like and what it reveals to us about the presence of God. Remember, the Tabernacle is the residence that God built for Himself.

1. **The Tabernacle (God's residence) consisted of a compound created by a fence. The Tabernacle compound had within it a smaller tent.**

2. **The Tabernacle compound (God's residence) measured roughly 23 metres by 46 metres.** The Tabernacle was a movable open-air courtyard created by a white linen fabric wall measuring twenty-three metres (50 cubits/75 feet) by forty-six metres (100 cubits/150 feet). The long side had twenty pillars and the short side had ten pillars.

> And thou shalt make the court of the tabernacle: for the south side southward there shall be hangings for the court of fine twined linen of AN HUNDRED CUBITS LONG FOR ONE SIDE: And the twenty pillars thereof and their twenty sockets shall be of brass; the hooks of the pillars and their fillets shall be of silver. And likewise for the north side in length there shall be hangings of an hundred cubits long, and his twenty pillars and their twenty sockets of brass; the hooks of the pillars and their fillets of silver.
>
> And for the breadth of the court on the west side shall be hangings of fifty cubits: their pillars ten, and their sockets ten. And the BREADTH OF THE COURT ON THE EAST SIDE EASTWARD SHALL BE FIFTY CUBITS.
>
> Exodus 27:9-13

3. **The Tabernacle compound (God's residence) had a fence around it. The fence was made of pillars and white linen curtains.**

And THOU SHALT MAKE THE COURT OF THE TABERNACLE: for the south side southward there shall be HANGINGS for the court OF FINE TWINED LINEN of an hundred cubits long for one side: And the twenty pillars thereof and their twenty sockets shall be of brass; the hooks of the pillars and their fillets shall be of silver. And likewise for the north side in length there shall be hangings of an hundred cubits long, and his twenty pillars and their twenty sockets of brass; the hooks of the pillars and their fillets of silver.

And for the breadth of the court on the west side shall be hangings of fifty cubits: THEIR PILLARS TEN, and their sockets ten. And the breadth of the court on the east side eastward shall be fifty cubits.

Exodus 27:9-13

4. **The Tabernacle compound (God's residence) had a nine-metre gate, composed of colourful linen, which opened into the large courtyard.** This gate was more like a curtain on five pillars than a modern gate that swings on hinges.

The gate of the courtyard is to have a thirty-foot screen embroidered with blue, purple, and scarlet yarn, and finely spun linen. It is to have four posts including their four bases.

Exodus 27:16 (HCSB)

5. **Ordinary Israelites were allowed to come to the gate of (God's residence) the open-air courtyard and present sacrifices.**

And the Lord called unto Moses, and spake unto him out of the Tabernacle of the congregation, saying, Speak unto the children of Israel, and say unto them, If any man of you bring an offering unto the Lord, ye shall bring your offering of the cattle, even of the herd, and of the flock. If his offering be a burnt sacrifice of the herd, let him offer a male without blemish: HE SHALL OFFER IT OF HIS OWN VOLUNTARY WILL AT THE DOOR OF THE TABERNACLE of the congregation before the Lord.

Leviticus 1:1-3

6. **Once inside the Tabernacle compound (the compound of God's residence), you would see an altar (for sacrifices), the laver (a wash-hand basin for hands and feet), and a small tent containing holier places.**

Then the Lord said to Moses, "Make A BRONZE BASIN, with its bronze stand, for washing. Place it BETWEEN THE TENT OF MEETING AND THE ALTAR, and put water in it. Aaron and his sons are to wash their hands and feet with water from it. Whenever they enter THE TENT OF MEETING, they shall wash with water so that they will not die. Also, when they approach the altar to minister by presenting an offering made to the Lord by fire, they shall wash their hands and feet so that they will not die. This is to be a lasting ordinance for Aaron and his descendants for the generations to come."

Exodus 30:17-21 (NIV)

7. **The Tabernacle (God's residence) had a small tent within it that measured 4.8 metres by 14 metres.** These measurements are deduced by calculating the size of panels in the Tabernacle.

Make The Dwelling itself from ten panels of tapestry woven from fine twisted linen, blue and purple and scarlet material, with an angel-cherubim design. A skilled craftsman should do it. The panels of tapestry are each to be forty-six feet long and six feet wide.

Exodus 26:1-2 (MSG)

8. **The Tabernacle (God's residence) had a small tent within it that had two rooms.** The first room was called the Holy Place and the second room was called the Holy of Holies.

Hang the veil under the clasps and bring the ark of the testimony there behind the veil, so the veil will make a separation for you between the holy place and the most holy place.

Exodus 26:33 (HCSB)

9. **The Tabernacle (God's residence) had a small tent within it and the door to this small tent was made up of five pillars.**

YOU SHALL MAKE A SCREEN FOR THE DOORWAY OF THE TENT of blue and purple and scarlet material and fine twisted linen, the work of a weaver. You shall make five pillars of acacia for the screen and overlay them with gold, their hooks also being of gold; and you shall cast five sockets of bronze for them.

Exodus 26:36-37 (NASB)

10. **The Holy Place was one of the small rooms within the small tent in God's residence.** It measured 4.8 metres by 9.1 metres. This measurement is deduced by calculating the size of the panels given in the book of Exodus.

11. **Ordinary priests were allowed to enter the first chamber (of God's residence) which was a covered tent called the Holy Place.**

In the Tabernacle of the congregation without the vail, which is before the testimony, Aaron and his sons shall order it from evening to morning before the Lord: it shall be a statute for ever unto their generations on the behalf of the children of Israel.

Exodus 27:21

12. **Once inside the Holy Place, you would see the Table of Shewbread, the Altar of Incense and the Candlestick.** Priests who entered the Holy Place had three items to deal with: the lamp, the incense and the table of holy bread.

They could burn the lamp, they could offer incense and they could eat the holy bread.

Hang the curtain from the clasps and place the ark of the Testimony behind the curtain. The curtain will separate the Holy Place from the Most Holy Place. Put the atonement cover on the ark of the Testimony in the Most Holy Place. Place THE TABLE outside the curtain on the north side of the Tabernacle and put THE LAMPSTAND opposite it on the south side.

Exodus 26:33-35 (NIV-MIT)

You are to make an ALTAR FOR THE BURNING OF INCENSE; make it of acacia wood. It must be square, 18 inches long and 18 inches wide; it must be 36 inches high. Its horns must be of one piece. Overlay its top, all around its sides, and its horns with pure gold; make a gold molding all around it. Make two gold rings for it under the molding on two of its sides; put these on opposite sides of it to be holders for the poles to carry it with. Make the poles of acacia wood and overlay them with gold.

You are to place the altar in front of the veil by the ark of the testimony — in front of the mercy seat that is over the testimony — where I will meet with you.

Aaron MUST BURN FRAGRANT INCENSE ON IT; he must burn it every morning when he tends the lamps. When Aaron sets up the lamps at twilight, he must burn incense. There is to be an incense offering before the Lord throughout your generations.

Exodus 30:1-8 (HCSB)

13. There was a veil that separated the Holy of Holies from the Holy Place in God's residence.

And THOU SHALT MAKE A VAIL OF BLUE, AND PURPLE, AND SCARLET, and fine twined linen of cunning work: with cherubims shall it be made: And thou shalt hang it upon four pillars of shittim wood overlaid with gold: their hooks shall be of gold, upon the four sockets of silver.

And thou shalt hang up the vail under the taches, that thou mayest bring in thither within the vail the ark of the testimony: AND THE VAIL SHALL DIVIDE UNTO YOU BETWEEN THE HOLY PLACE AND THE MOST HOLY.

Exodus 26:31-33

14. Inside the Holy of Holies of God's residence, there was a special piece of furniture called the Ark of the Covenant.

YOU SHALL MAKE POLES OF ACACIA WOOD AND OVERLAY THEM WITH GOLD. You shall put the poles into the rings on the sides of the ark, to carry the ark with them. The poles shall remain in the rings of the ark; they shall not be removed from it.

Exodus 25:13-15 (NASB)

15. In God's residence, only the High Priest was allowed to enter the Holy of Holies once a year.

Now when these things were thus ordained, the priests went always into the first tabernacle, accomplishing the service of God. BUT INTO THE SECOND WENT THE HIGH PRIEST ALONE ONCE EVERY YEAR, not without blood, which he offered for himself, and for the errors of the people:

Hebrews 9:6-7

CHAPTER 4

The Shadow of His Presence

For if he were on earth, he should not be a priest, seeing that there are priests that offer gifts according to the law: who serve unto the EXAMPLE and SHADOW OF HEAVENLY THINGS, AS MOSES WAS ADMONISHED OF GOD WHEN HE WAS ABOUT TO MAKE THE TABERNACLE: for, See, saith he, that thou make all things according to the pattern shewed to thee in the mount. But now hath he obtained a more excellent ministry, by how much also he is the mediator of a better covenant, which was established upon better promises.

For if that first covenant had been faultless, then should no place have been sought for the second.

Hebrews 8:4-7

The presence of God was seen in the Old Testament. In the Old Testament, God instituted the Tabernacle but this was just a shadow of the real thing. The real thing was yet to come. The Tabernacle was a foretaste of the real presence of God that you and I can experience if we are humble and open.

What does it mean for the Tabernacle to be a shadow? What does it mean for the Tabernacle to be a pattern? What does it mean for the Tabernacle to be a figure?

The components, the sections, the colours and the arrangement of the Tabernacle (God's residence) are a shadow of the things we need to do if we want to experience the presence of God. The examples of what to do in ministry, to invoke the presence of God, have been given to us. Through the things revealed in the Old Testament, we are shown how to find the presence of God today.

The Tabernacle (God's Old Testament residence) is the biggest revelation of the way into the presence of God. Keys to the presence of God will be revealed through the colours, items, furniture and their arrangement in the Tabernacle. In God's Old Testament residence, we have a marvellous guide to getting into the presence of God.

If you catch the revelation of the Tabernacle, you will have caught the secret to working in His presence. Your ministry is supposed to be lived out in the presence of God. God's presence is never supposed to depart from you. Through the revelation of the Tabernacle, God will show you how to live and to minister in the presence of God.

The book of Hebrews tells us that the Tabernacle is an example, a shadow and a pattern of things we are to do.

What does it mean for the Tabernacle to be an example to us? The Tabernacle represents something! The Tabernacle shows us something! The Tabernacle speaks to us about God and shows us truths we cannot receive in any other way. Through this book, you will find out about the presence of God and enjoy it. You will know how to dwell in the secret place of the Most High.

> **The Holy Ghost this signifying, that the way into the holiest of all was not yet made manifest, while as the first tabernacle was yet standing: Which was A FIGURE for the time then present, in which were offered both gifts and sacrifices, that could not make him that did the service perfect, as pertaining to the conscience;**
>
> **Hebrews 9:8-9**

1. **The Tabernacle, God's Old Testament residence is AN EXAMPLE of how to invoke the presence of God:** Examples show you things to imitate, things to follow and things to avoid.

   The Tabernacle is therefore an example showing you a ministry style that will bring on the presence of God.

   The Tabernacle is an example suggesting how your ministry should be if you are to experience the presence of God.

2. **The Tabernacle, God's Old Testament residence is A SHADOW of the presence of God:** Shadows sketch the outline of an object and show you the form of it.

   The Tabernacle is therefore a shadow showing you an outline of how to invoke the presence of God.

   The Tabernacle is a shadow sketching your ministry for you.

   The Tabernacle is a shadow that creates an image of how your ministry should be.

3. **The Tabernacle, God's Old Testament residence is A PATTERN of the presence of God:** Patterns give the shape, the impression, the style and show you the form of something.

The Tabernacle is an impression of what to do to have the presence of God.

The Tabernacle is a pattern of how to run your ministry.

4. **The Tabernacle, God's Old Testament residence is A FIGURE of the presence of God:** A figure is an image; a similitude of something.

   The Tabernacle is a parable that mysteriously sums up the keys to having the presence of God in your life and ministry.

   The Tabernacle is an illustration of how to have the presence of God.

CHAPTER 5

White Linen and God's Presence

Moreover THOU SHALT MAKE THE TABERNACLE WITH TEN CURTAINS OF FINE TWINED LINEN, and blue, and purple, and scarlet: with cherubims of cunning work shalt thou make them. The length of one curtain shall be eight and twenty cubits, and the breadth of one curtain four cubits: and every one of the curtains shall have one measure. The five curtains shall be coupled together one to another; and other five curtains shall be coupled one to another.

Exodus 26:1-3

White linen is the environment in which God dwells. White linen speaks of righteousness and holiness. Holiness and righteousness are essential if you are to attract the presence of God.

The fence of the Tabernacle was made of linen and the linen was white in colour. Many different items were used in the building of God's residence. Why was God so insistent on these different items with their different colours? Did they have any significance? Did white linen help to invoke the presence of God? It certainly did!

Colours do have symbolic meanings and we can learn these from the Bible. Wherever colours appear in the Bible, we can see and learn what they signify. Because fine linen is used in other parts of the Bible, we can also understand what linen signifies. The use of white linen in the Tabernacle is a revelation of how to create an environment that is conducive to the presence of God.

Do you want to have the presence of God in your ministry? Then you will need to have a lot of "white linen" which speaks of righteousness and holiness. If you do not build the Tabernacle according to the pattern, God will not inhabit it and His presence will not go with you in your ministry.

And he said, My presence shall go with thee, and I will give thee rest. And he said unto him, If thy presence go not with me, carry us not up hence.

Exodus 33:14-15

God's presence is found where there is righteousness. Holiness and righteousness are necessary if you want to experience God's presence. White linen speaks of righteousness, holiness and dedication to God. White was a colour that was used in the fence of the Tabernacle. The fence of the Tabernacle was made of linen and the linen was white in colour. White speaks of righteousness, holiness and dedication to God.

There is real righteousness in the presence of God. Without righteousness and holiness, you cannot see God!

Follow peace with all men, and holiness, without which no man shall see the Lord:

Hebrews 12:14

It is important to create a holy and righteous environment if you want to experience the presence of God. You can practically invoke the presence of God by creating a holy environment in which you will experience God's presence. A sin-ridden environment of wickedness, unrighteousness and evil will not invoke the presence of God.

In Scripture, White and Linen Speak of Righteousness and Holiness

The scripture is full of examples that use white and fine linen as a symbol of righteousness and holiness.

1. Let us be glad and rejoice, and give honour to him: for the marriage of the Lamb is come, and his wife hath made herself ready. And to her was granted that she should be arrayed in FINE LINEN, CLEAN AND WHITE: for the FINE LINEN IS THE RIGHTEOUSNESS OF SAINTS.

   Revelation 19:7-8

2. And when he knew it of the centurion, he gave the body to Joseph. And he bought FINE LINEN, and took him down, and wrapped him in the linen, and laid him in a sepulchre which was hewn out of a rock, and rolled a stone unto the door of the sepulchre.

   Mark 15:45-46

3. I beheld till the thrones were cast down, and THE ANCIENT OF DAYS DID SIT, WHOSE GARMENT WAS WHITE AS SNOW, and the hair of his head like the pure wool: his throne was like the fiery flame, and his wheels as burning fire.

   Daniel 7:9

4. And after six days Jesus taketh Peter, James, and John his brother, and bringeth them up into an high mountain apart, and was transfigured before them: and his face did shine as the sun, and HIS RAIMENT WAS WHITE AS THE LIGHT.

Matthew 17:1-2

CHAPTER 6

Scarlet and God's Presence

And thou shalt make an hanging for the door of the tent, of blue, and purple, and SCARLET, and fine twined linen, wrought with needlework.

Exodus 26:36

And for THE GATE OF THE COURT shall be an hanging of twenty cubits, of blue, and purple, and SCARLET, and fine twined linen, wrought with needlework: and their pillars shall be four, and their sockets four.

Exodus 27:16

And THOU SHALT MAKE A VAIL OF blue, and purple, and SCARLET, and fine twined linen of cunning work: with cherubims shall it be made:

Exodus 26:31

The use of scarlet in the Tabernacle (God's Old Testament residence) is a revelation of how to create an environment for the presence of God.

Without courage, you will not experience the presence of God. You need boldness to do the will of God. You need courage to pray for the sick and experience miracles. Without boldness you cannot walk in the manifestations of the Holy Spirit. Scarlet is always a sign of courage and boldness.

Scarlet was used in the building of the Tabernacle. Why was God so insistent on scarlet? Did it have any significance? Did scarlet help to invoke the presence of God? Yes, indeed it did! It was a clear pattern we were expected to follow.

Colours do have symbolic meanings and we can learn these from the Bible. Wherever the colours appear in the Bible, we can see and learn what they signify. Because the colour scarlet is used in other parts of the Bible, we can understand what it signifies. The use of scarlet in the Tabernacle is a revelation of how to create an environment that is conducive to the presence of God.

Scarlet speaks of courage and strength. Scarlet was a colour that was used in the gate, the door and the veil. The gate, the door and the veil of the Tabernacle were scarlet in colour. Scarlet speaks of courage and strength. It speaks of being a hero, valiant, courageous and fearless. This is the courage that is necessary to shed blood. Real courage and confidence is required to come boldly into the presence of God.

It is important to be bold if you want to experience the presence of God. You can practically invoke the presence of God by being bold and courageous in your preaching and your ministering. God's presence is always seen where there is boldness and clarity in the minister. Cowards do not deserve the presence of God. I once asked a prophet who was calling out names and numbers how he was able to do these things. He explained to me, "It takes ninety per cent of faith and boldness to minister as a prophet."

Indeed, without boldness, the presence of God is rarely experienced in a certain way. People who minister in the presence of God need to walk in boldness and fearlessness. You must not fear embarrassment. You must not be afraid of disgrace or humiliation. If you do not do the work of God with scarlet (boldness and courage), God's presence will not be manifest.

In Scripture, Scarlet Speaks of Courage and Strength

The scripture is full of examples that use scarlet as a symbol of courage and strength.

1. **Scarlet speaks of royal, kingly courage.**

> The shield of his mighty men is made red, THE VALIANT MEN ARE IN SCARLET: the chariots shall be with flaming torches in the day of his preparation, and the fir trees shall be terribly shaken.
>
> Nahum 2:3

2. **Scarlet speaks of courage to tell and speak the truth, even if it is against the powerful people of this world.** A person who has the presence of God is courageous and preaches the truth.

> The king cried aloud to bring in the astrologers, the Chaldeans, and the soothsayers. And the king spake, and said to the wise men of Babylon, WHOSOEVER SHALL READ THIS WRITING, AND SHEW ME THE INTERPRETATION THEREOF, SHALL BE CLOTHED WITH SCARLET, and have a chain of gold about his neck, and shall be the third ruler in the kingdom…
>
> And I have heard of thee, that thou canst make interpretations, and dissolve doubts: now IF THOU CANST READ THE WRITING, AND MAKE KNOWN TO ME THE INTERPRETATION THEREOF, THOU

SHALT BE CLOTHED WITH SCARLET, and have a chain of gold about thy neck, and shalt be the third ruler in the kingdom. Then Daniel answered and said before the king, Let thy gifts be to thyself, and give thy rewards to another; yet I will read the writing unto the king, and make known to him the interpretation…

And thou his son, O Belshazzar, hast not humbled thine heart, though thou knewest all this; But hast lifted up thyself against the Lord of heaven; and they have brought the vessels of his house before thee, and thou, and thy lords, thy wives, and thy concubines, have drunk wine in them; and thou hast praised the gods of silver, and gold, of brass, iron, wood, and stone, which see not, nor hear, nor know: and the God in whose hand thy breath is, and whose are all thy ways, hast thou not glorified:…

TEKEL; Thou art weighed in the balances, and art found wanting. PERES; Thy kingdom is divided, and given to the Medes and Persians. Then commanded Belshazzar, and THEY CLOTHED DANIEL WITH SCARLET, and put a chain of gold about his neck, and made a proclamation concerning him, that he should be the third ruler in the kingdom.

Daniel 5:7, 16-17, 22-23, 27-29

3. **Scarlet is a sign of courage.** Jesus demonstrated great courage in the presence of the wicked soldiers and enduring the crucifixion on the cross.

Then the soldiers of the governor took Jesus into the common hall, and gathered unto him the whole band of soldiers. And THEY STRIPPED HIM, AND PUT ON HIM A SCARLET ROBE.

Matthew 27:27-28

4. **Scarlet is a sign of fearlessness.** A virtuous woman is fearless. Many women are full of fear. A virtuous woman is not afraid of the next season. She is fearless in the event of snow.

She is not afraid of the snow for her household: for ALL HER HOUSEHOLD ARE CLOTHED WITH SCARLET.

Proverbs 31:21

5. **Scarlet is a sign of courage.** Scarlet is the ability to risk your life for Jesus Christ. Scarlet is the ability to risk everything for the work of God. Rahab risked her life when she helped the spies. She could have been tried and executed for treason. Rahab the harlot had the courage to help the spies and put out the scarlet thread.

Behold, when we come into the land, thou shalt bind this line of scarlet thread in the window which thou didst let us down by: and thou shalt bring thy father, and thy mother, and thy brethren, and all thy father's household, home unto thee. And it shall be, that whosoever shall go out of the doors of thy house into the street, his blood shall be upon his head, and we will be guiltless: and whosoever shall be with thee in the house, his blood shall be on our head, if any hand be upon him. And if thou utter this our business, then we will be quit of thine oath which thou hast made us to swear. And she said, according unto your words, so be it. And she sent them away, and they departed: and SHE BOUND THE SCARLET LINE IN THE WINDOW.

Joshua 2:18-21

6. **Scarlet is a sign of boldness.** Pharez came out first. It takes great courage to lead the way. It takes even greater courage to do something that no one else has done. When you come out first, there is no one in front of you. Coming out first when there is no example before you, takes courage indeed.

And it came to pass, when she travailed, that the one put out his hand: and THE MIDWIFE TOOK AND BOUND UPON HIS HAND A SCARLET THREAD, saying, This came out first.

And it came to pass, as he drew back his hand, that, behold, his brother came out: and she said, How hast thou broken forth? This breach be upon thee: therefore his name was called Pharez. And afterward came out his brother, that had the scarlet thread upon his hand: and his name was called Zarah.

Genesis 38:28-30

CHAPTER 7

Purple and God's Presence

And for THE GATE OF THE COURT SHALL BE AN HANGING OF twenty cubits, of blue, and PURPLE, and scarlet, and fine twined linen, wrought with needlework: and their pillars shall be four, and their sockets four.

Exodus 27:16

And thou shalt make an hanging FOR THE DOOR OF THE TENT, of blue, and PURPLE, and scarlet, and fine twined linen, wrought with needlework.

Exodus 26:36

And thou shalt make A VAIL OF blue, and PURPLE, and scarlet, and fine twined linen of cunning work: with cherubims shall it be made:

Exodus 26:31

Moreover thou shalt make the Tabernacle with ten curtains of fine twined linen, and blue, and PURPLE, and scarlet: with cherubims of cunning work shalt thou make them.

Exodus 26:1

Make sure the environment of your church has a royal feel. A royal feel is necessary for the presence of God.

Purple was used in the building of the Tabernacle. God was insistent on purple because it is a great example and pattern of what God wants and what He does not want. Purple was one of the colours that was used abundantly in the Tabernacle.

The colour purple helps to invoke the presence of God. Colours do have symbolic meanings and we can learn these from the Bible. Wherever the colours appear in the Bible, we can see and learn what they signify. We can learn what these colours speak of by studying the scripture and noting what the scripture says about them.

A shabby, dirty, poverty-stricken environment does not encourage the presence of God.

You must create a royal environment if you want to experience the presence of God. You must build the Tabernacle according to the pattern God has given. You must use purple to bring in the presence of God! God wants to see purple! God is comfortable in the presence of royalty! God will not inhabit places that do not have a royal feel. By using purple, His presence will go everywhere with you. Your ministry will be power-packed with the presence of God.

And he said, My presence shall go with thee, and I will give thee rest. And he said unto him, If thy presence go not with me, carry us not up hence.

Exodus 33:14-15

Purple speaks of royalty. Purple was a colour that was used in the gate, the door and the veil of the Tabernacle. Purple speaks of riches, wealth and royalty. Indeed, there are riches, wealth and royalty in the presence of God.

It is important to create a royal environment if you want to experience the presence of God. You can practically invoke the presence of God by creating a royal environment in which you will experience God's presence. A ramshackle, poverty-stricken, broken down and bedraggled environment will not invoke the presence of God. A rickety, impoverished, unkempt environment will only evoke feelings of depression and discouragement.

In Scripture, Purple Speaks of Riches and Royalty

The scripture is full of examples that use purple as a symbol of riches and royalty. Lydia was a seller of purple because purple was something valuable to be bought.

1. **Purple is a sign of riches and prosperity.** Lydia was a seller of purple. She was a successful woman in the city. God is not against success and riches. Your success and your riches must be turned towards God. You must honour God with your success. There is nothing wrong with doing business and trading. You must remember God and honour Him with what He gives you.

And a certain woman named Lydia, A SELLER OF PURPLE, of the city of Thyatira, which worshipped God, heard us: whose heart the Lord opened, that she attended unto the things which were spoken of Paul. And when she was baptized, and her household, she besought us, saying, if ye have judged me to be faithful to the Lord, come into my house, and abide there. And she constrained us.

Acts 16:14-15

2. **The rich man who went to hell was clothed in purple.** He was completely covered with this sign of riches. The rich man did not go to hell because he was rich. Abraham, who was in heaven, was also a rich man when he was on earth. It is important that you use the riches and the royalty that you have to the glory of God. In the presence of God, there are riches and royalty. God is not averse to wealth. It is wealthy people who turn away from Him because of their little prosperity. Do not clothe yourself with riches and royalty in such a way that you forget God!

There was a certain RICH MAN, WHICH WAS CLOTHED IN PURPLE and fine linen, and fared sumptuously every day:

Luke 16:19

3. **King Solomon was clothed in purple.** As you can see, purple is a sign of real riches and royalty. Genuine riches and royalty come from God. It is God who made Solomon the richest man who ever lived. There are riches and divine promotion in the presence of God. As you walk in God's presence, you can expect to receive riches and divine promotion.

King Solomon made himself a chariot of the wood of Lebanon. He made the pillars thereof of silver, the bottom thereof of gold, THE COVERING OF IT OF PURPLE, the midst thereof being paved with love, for the daughters of Jerusalem.

Song of Solomon 3:9-10

4. **The kings of Midian had purple raiment.** Purple is a kingly colour. You can expect to receive kingly promotion in the presence of God. As you serve God in the ministry, He will make you like a king. Many people will serve you. Your brethren will come and bow down to you. The presence of God brings honour into your life.

And the weight of the golden earrings that he requested was a thousand and seven hundred shekels of gold; beside ornaments, and collars, and PURPLE RAIMENT THAT WAS ON THE KINGS OF MIDIAN, and beside the chains that were about their camels' necks.

Judges 8:26

5. **Jesus was clothed with purple when He was being crucified.** Purple was the sign that they were dealing with someone unusual. Jesus was true royalty. Even His enemies acknowledged His royalty as they crucified Him. Make sure the environment of your church has a royal feel. The proper lighting, the proper colours and the proper atmosphere all help to bring about the presence of God.

And the soldiers led him away into the hall, called Praetorium; and they call together the whole band. And THEY CLOTHED HIM WITH PURPLE, and platted a crown of thorns, and put it about his head, AND BEGAN TO SALUTE HIM, HAIL, KING OF THE JEWS!

Mark 15:16-18

6. **The virtuous woman wore purple.** Shabbily dressed women are not attractive. Shabby women do not attract men into their lives. That is why girls spend so much money on clothes and dresses. A good woman dresses well and makes herself attractive. Indeed, purple attracts the presence of God. Be smart! Be well dressed! Be neat! Look beautiful! Look nice! It all helps as you seek to enjoy the presence of God. Shabby, ill-matched clothes breed an atmosphere of discouragement and disillusionment. When the ladies in the church are not smart, it affects the atmosphere. If you are met at the church door by a dishevelled untidy woman, you are not likely to feel the presence of God.

She maketh herself coverings of tapestry; HER CLOTHING IS SILK AND PURPLE.

Proverbs 31:22

7. **The great city was clothed in purple.** A great church will have the marks of royalty all over. Royalty helps to bring in the presence of God.

And saying, Alas, alas, THAT GREAT CITY, THAT WAS CLOTHED in fine linen, AND PURPLE, and scarlet, and decked with gold, and precious stones, and pearls! For in one hour so great riches is come to nought…

Revelation 18:16-17

CHAPTER 8

Blue and God's Presence

And shall put thereon the covering of badgers 'skins, and shall spread over it A CLOTH WHOLLY OF BLUE, and shall put in the staves thereof.

And upon the table of shewbread they shall spread A CLOTH OF BLUE, and put thereon the dishes, and the spoons, and the bowls, and covers to cover withal: and the continual bread shall be thereon:

And they shall take A CLOTH OF BLUE, and cover the candlestick of the light, and his lamps, and his tongs, and his snuffdishes, and all the oil vessels thereof, wherewith they minister unto it:

And upon the golden altar they shall spread A CLOTH OF BLUE, and cover it with a covering of badgers' skins, and shall put to the staves thereof:

And they shall take all the instruments of ministry, wherewith they minister in the sanctuary, and put them in A CLOTH OF BLUE, and cover them with a covering of badgers 'skins, and shall put them on a bar.

Numbers 4:6-7, 9, 11-12

Blue was used in the building of the Tabernacle. Why was God so insistent on these different colours? Did it have any significance? Did the colour blue help to invoke the presence of God? Yes indeed, it did! It was a clear pattern we were expected to follow.

Blue does have a symbolic meaning and we can learn about it from the Bible. Wherever the colours appear in the Bible, we can see and learn what they signify. Because the colour blue is used in other parts of the Bible, we can understand what it signifies. The use of blue in the Tabernacle is a revelation of how to create an environment that is conducive to the presence of God.

Sapphire stone is best known as a blue stone and wherever you see sapphire, you can assume you are seeing a classic blue colour. "Above the dome there was something that looked like a throne, SKY-BLUE LIKE A SAPPHIRE, with a human-like figure towering above the throne" (Ezekiel 1:26, Message Bible).

Sapphire, the most precious blue gem stone, is mentioned often in the scripture in relation to God. It is seen as a stone of COMMITMENT, WISDOM AND Rne OYALTY. Indeed, rulers of ancient Persia believed the sky was painted blue by the reflection of sapphire stones. Sapphire is the holy stone of the Catholic Church and indeed many religions believe that the blue sapphire represents the heavens.

There is stability, faithfulness and commitment in the presence of God. The loyalty of Mordecai was rewarded with royal blue. The character of the king is the character of wisdom and loyalty. When a king speaks a word, you can trust that it will come to pass. The word of the king is sure.

Blue speaks of stability, loyalty, service to God and faithfulness. Blue was a colour that was used in the coverings of the tent, the table of shewbread, the candlestick, the altar and other instruments in the Tabernacle.

All those who are used by God must be faithful. Their words must be sure. There must be no sudden change in you. You must be somebody who is loyal and who cannot easily change his position.

It is important to be stable, faithful and loyal if you want to experience the presence of God. You can practically invoke the presence of God by being in the service of God with a faithful heart. A treacherous person will not invoke the presence of God.

If you do not develop your ministry using royal faithfulness and commitment, you will not see the presence of God. God will not inhabit your ministry and His presence will not go far with you if loyalty, faithfulness and stability are discarded. You may start well but you will need faithfulness to maintain the presence of God for the long haul.

In Scripture, Blue Speaks of Commitment, Stability and Faithfulness

The scripture is full of examples that use blue or sapphire as a symbol of awesome royalty, commitment, stability and faithfulness.

1. **Faithful Mordecai who exposed traitors and disloyal people was clothed in blue.**

> And MORDECAI WENT OUT FROM THE PRESENCE OF THE KING IN ROYAL APPAREL OF BLUE AND WHITE, and with a great crown of gold, and with a garment of fine linen and purple: and the city of Shushan rejoiced and was glad.
>
> Esther 8:15

Mordecai was clothed in blue as a sign of his faithfulness. The king's life was spared because of this faithful man. Commitment and faithfulness are essential for God's work. It is required in stewards that a man be found faithful (1 Corinthians 4:2). God expects divine stability and loyalty from those who serve Him. Faithfulness in a church is necessary for the presence of God. Churches which are full of quarrels, confusion and strife do not have the presence of God.

2. Above the four living creatures in the firmament, is blue like sapphire.

> And I looked, and, behold, a whirlwind came out of the north, a great cloud, and a fire infolding itself, and a brightness was about it, and out of the midst thereof as the colour of amber, out of the midst of the fire. Also out of the midst thereof came the likeness of four living creatures.
>
> And this was their appearance; they had the likeness of a man.... AND ABOVE THE FIRMAMENT THAT WAS OVER THEIR HEADS WAS THE LIKENESS OF A THRONE, AS THE APPEARANCE OF A SAPPHIRE STONE: and upon the likeness of the throne was the likeness as the appearance of a man above upon it.
>
> Ezekiel 1:4-5, 26

Ezekiel saw a vision of four living creatures. These are stable, faithful, loyal creatures that hover around the throne of God. Their appearance is like the sapphire stone. Remember that sapphire is a blue precious stone. Sapphire is often synonymous with the colour blue. To experience the presence of God, we need people who are stable, eternal and permanent.

3. Above the cherubim in the firmament, is blue like a sapphire stone.

> Then I looked, and, behold, in the firmament that was above the head of the cherubims there appeared over them as it were a sapphire stone, as the appearance of the likeness of a throne.
>
> Ezekiel 10:1

The blue in the firmament above, speaks of the loyalty and permanence of God's throne. God's throne is immovable and permanent no matter what happens on the earth. As you become immovable and permanent in ministry, you will experience the power and presence of God. People who are unstable and unfaithful do not attract the presence of God.

4. Moses, Aaron, Nadab and Abihu saw God sitting on a blue sapphire pavement.

Then went up Moses, and Aaron, Nadab, and Abihu, and seventy of the elders of Israel: And they saw the God of Israel: and THERE WAS UNDER HIS FEET AS IT WERE A PAVED WORK OF A SAPPHIRE STONE, AND AS IT WERE THE BODY OF HEAVEN IN HIS CLEARNESS. And upon the nobles of the children of Israel he laid not his hand: also they saw God, and did eat and drink. And the Lord said unto Moses, Come up to me into the mount, and be there: and I will give thee tables of stone, and a law, and commandments which I have written; that thou mayest teach them.

Exodus 24:9-12

God is greater than we can ever imagine. His presence is found on top of a blue sapphire pavement. Blue is a very important colour to God. That is the colour on which God sets His throne. It is the colour of stability, loyalty and faithfulness. Fight for loyalty, faithfulness and stability in your ministry and you will experience the greatness of His presence in your life. Would you not like to see the greatness of God sitting on a pavement of heavenly blue? You will see this wonderful presence as you develop divine loyalty, faithfulness and stability.

5. The instruments of God are covered in a cloth of blue.

And UPON THE GOLDEN ALTAR THEY SHALL SPREAD A CLOTH OF BLUE, and cover it with a covering of badgers' skins, and shall put to the staves thereof: And THEY SHALL TAKE ALL THE INSTRUMENTS OF MINISTRY, wherewith they minister in the sanctuary, and PUT THEM IN A CLOTH OF BLUE, and cover them with a covering of badgers' skins, and shall put them on a bar:

Numbers 4:11-12

Every person who is used by God must be covered in a blue cloth of loyalty and faithfulness. After being covered in the blue cloth they are put on the altar. The blue cloth speaks of the loyalty and constancy that must characterize your calling and ministry. A person who can be faithful to his original calling will experience the presence of God. Many ministers have veered off from preaching the word of God into vain jangling. You will not believe how ministers are teaching economics, business and money management instead of being faithful to the original call of God.

6. The blueness of a wound speaks of healing.

> **THE BLUENESS OF A WOUND CLEANSETH AWAY EVIL: so do stripes the inward parts of the belly.**
>
> **Proverbs 20:30**

Everyone is wounded in the battle of ministry. Unfortunately, some people are never healed of their wounds. As wounds fester, other evils come in. Hatred, bitterness and evil thoughts sprout where there are unhealed wounds. The blueness of a wound speaks of the healing of that wound. The blueness of your wound speaks of your stability and immovability.

The blueness of your wound therefore speaks of your resistance to being pushed away and being set aside by hurts and offences.

Hurts and offences are well known causes of disloyalty and unfaithfulness. As you grow in stability and faithfulness, nothing will be able to move you. Your wounds will all turn blue and you will recover completely from the hurts of life and ministry. You will experience the presence of God as you grow in "blue" faithfulness, loyalty, stability, dependability and constancy!

CHAPTER 9

Gold and God's Presence

And they shall make an ark of shittim wood: two cubits and a half shall be the length thereof, and a cubit and a half the breadth thereof, and a cubit and a half the height thereof.

And THOU SHALT OVERLAY IT WITH PURE GOLD, within and without shalt thou overlay it, and shalt MAKE UPON IT A CROWN OF GOLD ROUND ABOUT. And thou shalt cast four rings of gold for it, and put them in the four corners thereof; and two rings shall be in the one side of it, and two rings in the other side of it.

Exodus 25:10-12

YOU SHALL MAKE POLES OF ACACIA WOOD AND OVERLAY THEM WITH GOLD. You shall put the poles into the rings on the sides of the ark, to carry the ark with them.

Exodus 25:13-14 (NASB)

THOU SHALT ALSO MAKE A TABLE OF SHITTIM WOOD: two cubits shall be the length thereof, and a cubit the breadth thereof, and a cubit and a half the height thereof. AND THOU SHALT OVERLAY IT WITH PURE GOLD, and make thereto a crown of gold round about.

Exodus 25:23-24

You shall make A MERCY SEAT OF PURE GOLD, two and a half cubits long and one and a half cubits wide.

Exodus 25:17 (NASB)

And THOU SHALT MAKE TWO CHERUBIMS OF GOLD, of beaten work shalt thou make them, in the two ends of the mercy seat.

Exodus 25:18

Gold was used and specified by the Lord in the building of the Tabernacle. Was gold chosen for its colour or its durability? Or was there some other reason? I believe that gold was chosen by God as an example, a pattern and a shadow of what attracts the presence of God.

Wherever God dwells, there must be these patterns, colours and symbols. These patterns, colours and materials create a certain environment that God can dwell in. Most of the colours and metals indicate the presence of kingly characteristics. Kingly characteristics always have strength, authority, faithfulness, wealth, judgment, security and gifts.

If you want to build or create a place where God will dwell (mishkan) then you must get these things. Spend your effort and time to create a golden environment.

Gold speaks of an eternal and precious treasure! Gold was used in the Holy Place and in the Holy of Holies. Gold speaks of lasting valuable treasures and precious things. There is an eternal and precious treasure in the presence of God.

Gold was a precious treasure used to create a meeting place for the presence of God. Indeed, there are eternal riches and wealth in the presence of God. It is important to create a precious environment if you want to experience the presence of God.

If you do not build the Tabernacle according to the gold pattern, God will not inhabit it and His presence will not go with you in your ministry.

In the Scriptures, Gold Speaks of a Valuable Treasure

The scripture is full of examples that use gold as a symbol of eternal value and great treasure.

1. **Gold speaks of something eternal as against the temporary things we have on earth.**

> **Now if any man build upon this foundation gold, silver, precious stones, wood, hay, stubble; Every man's work shall be made manifest: for the day shall declare it, because it shall be revealed by fire; and the fire shall try every man's work of what sort it is.**
>
> **1 Corinthians 3:12-13**

Today, many ministries are earthly-minded. Pastors preach about business all the time. Conventions are held to encourage business, politics and every other earthly endeavour. In so doing, the church has lost value. Instead of preaching about the cross of Jesus Christ, the blood of Jesus and the love of God, ministers of God are explaining terms like "the accounting rate of return, net realisable values, depreciation of non-current assets, valuation of inventories, window-dressing, liquidity ratios, amortization, leverage, financial engineering and securitization of future earnings." All these "word salads" are not valuable in the sight of God.

Where is eternity in the teachings of today's church? Why don't Christians teach about heaven and its rewards? Why don't preachers talk about the punishment of hell anymore? The gold of the Tabernacle has been replaced with a shiny metal that has no value. Pastors want to be motivational speakers instead of gospel preachers! Men of God have set aside teachings about heaven and hell. Today, people only preach about having a good life, a good family, a good marriage, a good business and good children. Many psychologists could easily replace pastors in their pulpits. It is time to go back for the gold. Let's talk about eternity! Let's talk about our eternal rewards! Let's talk about working for God! The gospel must be preached. Churches must be planted. The words of Jesus must be obeyed!

People who preach about eternity experience the presence of God in their lives. People who are focused on eternity experience the presence of God. Gold is necessary if you want to experience the presence of God.

2. Gold speaks of something durable and tested, something that survives!

But he knoweth the way that I take: WHEN HE HATH TRIED ME, I SHALL COME FORTH AS GOLD.

Job 23:10

Blessed are those who overcome many tests and trials. The presence of God is where such people are. Gold is a symbol of your ability to survive tests and trials. Many people fall away when they are tested. Gold speaks of the ability to survive tests. When you have been through tests, trials and temptations, you come out with a gold colour. That colour indicates that you are a survivor and an overcomer. The power of God is found with survivors.

3. Gold speaks of glory and beauty.

The king's daughter is all glorious within: her clothing is of wrought gold.

Psalms 45:13

Gold speaks of beauty and glory. The glory of God needs to be in your life and ministry. Where the glory is, the presence will be! How can you have this glory? You can have glory when you bear much fruit. "Herein is my Father glorified, that ye bear much fruit; so shall ye be my disciples." (John 15:8). Much fruit brings in the glory of God. Do you want to see the glory of God? Then bear much fruit! Do not bear a little fruit! Decide to be very fruitful! Fruitfulness releases glory and glory is the gold that will bring down the presence of God.

4. Gold speaks of something precious, everlasting and expensive treasure.

And I will punish the world for their evil, and the wicked for their iniquity; and I will cause the arrogancy of the proud to cease, and will lay low the haughtiness of the terrible. I will make a man MORE PRECIOUS THAN FINE GOLD; even a man than the golden wedge of Ophir.

Isaiah 13:11-12

Gold is precious. Souls are precious to God! Euros and dollars are not precious to God. Many things that are highly esteemed of men are valueless in the sight of God. There are ministries that look impressive in terms of size and volume. In actual fact, they may be very unimpressive to God. You may have a ministry that is only worth a truck full of wood and hay and feel that you are the greatest on earth. But somebody's tiny wedding ring may be worth far more than your truck full of hay and wood.

Indeed, some people's small ministries are more precious than some super impressive, voluminous and loud ministries. Aim to do things that are truly precious to God. What does God value? God does not value your big car nor does He value your shiny expensive suits. God values souls. Souls are precious to God. One soul is worth more than the whole world. If you give yourself to soul winning, you are giving yourself to something that is truly precious and valuable. Those who win souls have the presence of God. Soul winners have the gold in their ministries.

He shall stretch forth his hand also upon the countries: and the land of Egypt shall not escape. But he shall have power over THE TREASURES OF GOLD and of silver, and OVER ALL THE PRECIOUS THINGS of Egypt: and the Libyans and the Ethiopians shall be at his steps.

Daniel 11:42-43

CHAPTER 10

Brass and God's Presence

And THOU SHALT MAKE FIFTY TACHES OF BRASS, and put the taches into the loops, and couple the tent together, that it may be one.

Exodus 26:11

Brass signifies strength! Do these different metals help to invoke the presence of God? Different metals have symbolic meanings and we can learn this from the Bible. Brass was used in the outer court, whilst gold was used in the holy places. Brass was used in the making of the joints of the tent.

Wherever these shiny metals appear in the Bible, we can learn what they signify. Because brass is used in other parts of the Bible, we can understand what it signifies. The use of brass in the Tabernacle is a revelation of how to create an environment that is conducive to the presence of God.

You must build with brass. Brass signifies strength. God will not inhabit places that do not have brass. Brass signifies strength and force. Without brass, His presence will not be with you in your ministry. You will not have rest in the ministry if you do not use brass. "And he said, My presence shall go with thee, and I will give thee rest. And he said unto him, If thy presence go not with me, carry us not up hence" (Exodus 33:14-15).

Without strength you cannot rule people! Without strength you cannot lead! Without strength you cannot take decisions that are necessary for the improvement of the church. The presence of brass in the Tabernacle reveals the presence of strong character and strength of purpose.

Brass speaks of kingly strength, suffering and judgment.

Brass was a precious treasure used to create a meeting place for the presence of God. Indeed, there is strength in the presence of God.

It is important to create God's residential environment if you want to experience the presence of God. You can practically invoke the presence of God by being strong and yet open to suffering and judgment. An environment characterised by weakness will not invoke the presence of God.

You cannot create a good church or a good ministry without strength. People think that strength is offensive but strength is necessary for the presence of God. Weak leaders cause division by their style of leadership. Weak leaders cause disloyalty to arise because of their style of leadership. I can often point the start of confusion to weak leadership and poor leadership skills.

In the Scriptures, Brass Speaks of Kingly Strength, Suffering and Judgment

The scripture is full of examples that use brass as a symbol of strength.

1. Brass speaks of a conquering power.

> Arise and thresh, O daughter of Zion: for I will make thine horn iron, and I WILL MAKE THY HOOFS BRASS: AND THOU SHALT BEAT IN PIECES MANY PEOPLE: and I will consecrate their gain unto the Lord, and their substance unto the Lord of the whole earth.
>
> Micah 4:13

God is making your hoofs brass. He is taking away your weak and phlegmatic nature and giving you hoofs of brass. Through this conquering power, you will plant churches and take territories for Jesus Christ. Through conquering power, you will go from nation to nation doing the work of God. Through conquering power, you will crush all forms of disloyalty in your ministry.

Fearless strength will characterize your decisions. You will move forward in spite of opposition, resistance and accusation. When you walk in the strength of God, you set aside your human weakness. Through divine strength, you will accomplish great things in the name of the Lord.

Do not be a weakling! Do not be ruled by human opinion! Do not be ruled by the fear of man! Do not be ruled by your wife!

Do not be ruled by your assistants! Be a strong leader! Without this kind of strength, you will not experience the presence of God in your life and ministry.

2. Brass speaks of an unyielding power.

> The Lord shall smite thee with a consumption, and with a fever, and with an inflammation, and with an extreme burning, and with the sword, and with blasting, and with mildew; and they shall pursue thee until thou perish. And THY HEAVEN THAT IS OVER THY HEAD SHALL BE BRASS, and the earth that is under thee shall be iron.
>
> Deuteronomy 28:22-23

The heavens that refuse to yield rain are called the heavens of brass. No matter the prayers, the pleadings and the hopes of the people, there is simply no rain, no dew and no water. Brass, therefore, speaks of an unyielding strength which does not back down. In the presence of God, there is unyielding power, unyielding strength. Refuse to give up! Refuse to go back! Refuse to back down on your calling! Such qualities and such attitudes please God. They will attract His presence.

John the Baptist was an unyielding minister. Jesus spoke about him and said John the Baptist was not a reed shaken by the wind. John the Baptist was unyielding. That was why he carried the presence of God. He could not be moved by the pressure of society. He was not moved by the fear of man. He was committed to being a voice in the wilderness.

Can you be turned back from your calling by your mother or your auntie? Does your wife guide you and lead you? If so, you are nothing but a wimp! Can your wife make you resign from the ministry? Can she dictate the next step to you? If the answer is "Yes" you do not have hoofs of brass. You must become a heaven of brass, unyielding and never giving up.

Stop being double-minded from today!

3. Brass speaks of an indestructible power.

> His bones are as STRONG PIECES OF BRASS; his bones are like bars of iron.
>
> Job 40:18

To do the work of ministry, you need to have strong bones. Your bones must be like strong pieces of brass. When your bones are like brass and iron, you are indestructible. In the ministry, many things will seek to destroy you. There are many strong enemies that are training to come against you. Weaklings will not survive in the battle of ministry. Expect to have attacks of pride, bitterness, unforgiveness, lust, discouragement and depression. Goliath came out against David, covered with brass. He planned to destroy David. That is how enemies will come out against you. You must equally strengthen your bones in readiness for all attacks.

> And there went out a champion out of the camp of the Philistines, named Goliath, of Gath, whose height was six cubits and a span. And he had AN HELMET OF BRASS upon his head, and he was armed with a coat of mail; and the weight of the coat was five thousand shekels of brass. And he had GREAVES OF BRASS UPON HIS LEGS, and a TARGET OF BRASS BETWEEN HIS SHOULDERS.
>
> 1 Samuel 17:4-6

All the rewards in the book of Revelation are for those who overcome. Today, you are receiving the quality of brass into your life. You will overcome all types of Goliaths that are sent to you. Fighting with the "brass" kind of strength attracts the presence of God. The power of God accompanied David as he fought against Goliath. That is how the presence of God will be with you when you gird your loins with strength and fight against God's enemies.

4. Brass speaks of binding power.

> And she said, The Philistines be upon thee, Samson. And he awoke out of his sleep, and said, I will go out as at other

> times before, and shake myself. And he wist not that the Lord was departed from him. BUT THE PHILISTINES TOOK HIM, and put out his eyes, and brought him down to Gaza, AND BOUND HIM WITH FETTERS OF BRASS; and he did grind in the prison house.
>
> Judges 16:20-21

Brass speaks of binding power. Samson was bound with brass. Samson was restrained with brass. Brass speaks of power to restrain an enemy. The Tabernacle was built with brass. The presence of God is found where you restrain the enemy.

It is important to learn how to bind satan. You must use a lot of binding power to resist evil spirits. It is important for you to bind devils regularly, frequently and for long hours. Devils are real and they have surrounded you, intending to destroy you. Believe in their existence and bind them regularly! They will hate you for it and they will hate you for remembering that they are there. They will beg to be relieved of their assignment to torment you.

Bind the spirit of opposition! Bind the spirit of accusation! Bind the spirit that takes away your rest! Bind the spirit that is sent to wear you out! Bind the spirit of temptation! Bind the spirit of death! Bind the spirit of Jezebel! Bind the spirit of manipulation! Bind the spirit of evil counsel! Bind the spirit of adultery! Bind the spirit of pornography! Bind the spirit of deception!

CHAPTER 11

Silver and God's Presence

And thou shalt make forty SOCKETS OF SILVER under the twenty boards; two sockets under one board for his two tenons, and two sockets under another board for his two tenons.

Exodus 26:19

You shall make the court of the Tabernacle. On the south side there shall be hangings for the court of fine twisted linen one hundred cubits long for one side; and its pillars shall be twenty, with their twenty sockets of bronze; the hooks of the pillars and THEIR BANDS SHALL BE OF SILVER.

Exodus 27:9-10 (NASB)

Silver was used extensively in the building of the Tabernacle (God's holy residence).

Silver speaks of redemption by God. Silver was a precious treasure used to create a meeting place for the presence of God. Silver was used in the pillars and the sockets of the Tabernacle. There is redemption in the presence of God. Silver, God's redeeming power, was used extensively in the building of the Tabernacle.

Indeed, many different metals were used in the building of the Tabernacle. Why was God so insistent on these different elements? Why did He not just use brass or wood? What is the significance of silver? Did the different metals in the Tabernacle mean anything?

Indeed, different metals have symbolic meanings and we can learn all this from the Bible.

Wherever precious minerals appear in the Bible, they have great significance. The use of silver in other parts of the Bible teach us a lot. The use of silver in the Tabernacle is a revelation of how to create an environment that God loves.

You must build with silver! Silver signifies redemption! God will not inhabit the places that do not have silver. Silver speaks of how God redeems and utterly saves sinners. Silver speaks of how God utterly purchases people from the hands of the wicked. Without redemption, you will not have most of the people you are supposed to have in your ministry and the presence of God will not be there.

To redeem something is to buy something. "Redeem" is an old word which simply means to purchase something. You could say, "I am going to the shopping mall to redeem a few things." What you actually mean is that, "I am going to the mall to buy a few things." We are not worthy to be in the house of God. There had to be a serious transaction to legally import us into the church of Jesus Christ.

Through God's active redeeming power, many, many people are added to the house of God. The many grateful people who are redeemed, create an atmosphere which brings the presence of God. Today, the church is filled with terrible sinners who know that they deserve to go to hell. The church is filled with people who are just thankful to have their names in the Book of Life. The church is filled with people who still continue to sin because they are helplessly programmed to follow their flesh. And yet, all these people are redeemed or purchased by God at great price. God values each and every soul who gathers at His feet.

Redemption is the manifestation of forgiveness and great mercies. Without the strength that redemption brings, there would be no one in the house of God. The redeemed of the Lord are very grateful. They gather to praise the God who has shown them mercy. It is important to believe in God's redemption if you want to experience the presence of God. You can practically invoke the presence of God by believing in the atoning blood of Jesus.

If you do not build the church with the silver pattern, God will not inhabit it and His presence will not go with you in your ministry. If you do not accept sinners who are equally purchased and set free by the blood of the Lamb, you will have a very different church and a very different environment. Do you want to experience the presence of God? Then you need to believe in redemption! You need to believe in forgiveness! You need to believe in restoration!

The television that should have been in the shop is now legally in your house because you bought (redeemed) it. The souls that should have been in hell are now legally in the house of God because they have been bought (redeemed) by the blood of the Lamb.

Churches that have few people have a different atmosphere and a different feeling. Churches that have many people have an atmosphere that is beautiful and also powerful. That powerful atmosphere is the presence of God that comes from the presence of multitudes of unworthy but legally redeemed people.

In the Scriptures, Silver Speaks of Redemption

The scripture is full of examples that use silver as a symbol of redemption.

1. Silver is the prophetic price of redemption.

And I said unto them, if ye think good, give me my price; and if not, forbear. So THEY WEIGHED FOR MY PRICE THIRTY PIECES OF SILVER.

Zechariah 11:12

Silver speaks of salvation and redemption. Where Christians preach about salvation and redemption, the presence of God is felt. You will not feel the presence of God when you hear preaching on entrepreneurship, free enterprise and gross domestic products. The presence of God comes where redemption and salvation are prominent.

The prophet prophesied of Jesus being sold for thirty pieces of silver. His life was given for thirty pieces of silver. Prophetically, silver speaks of redemption. Silver was used to pay for Jesus' life. In other words, silver was used to pay for all our lives.

2. Silver was the price for Jesus to save our lives and redeem us.

Wherefore that field was called, the field of blood, unto this day. Then was fulfilled that which was spoken by Jeremy the prophet, saying, And they took the THIRTY PIECES OF SILVER, THE PRICE OF HIM THAT WAS VALUED, whom they of the children of Israel did value:

Matthew 27:8-9

Salvation is the most important subject in the world today. God sent Jesus to be the Saviour of the world. He was to save us from our sins. The more we preach about this salvation the more we will experience the presence of God.

I once listened to a great man of God preaching the word of God. I enjoyed his message and was blessed greatly. After some years, I could no longer listen to even a few minutes of this same man's preaching. I thought to myself, "It is just one of those things." After some time however, I found out that this man had veered off from mainline gospel preaching into other things. He even began to make a mockery of salvation, redemption and the blood of Jesus. I then understood why his preaching had lost its impact in my life. I no longer experienced the presence of God when he taught. Silver, which speaks of redemption, salvation and restoration is a key element if we want to experience the presence of God.

3. Silver was the price used to pay for the life of Joseph who saved Israel.

Come, and let us sell him to the Ishmeelites, and let not our hand be upon him; for he is our brother and our flesh. And his brethren were content. Then there passed by Midianites merchantmen; and they drew and lifted up Joseph out of the pit, AND SOLD JOSEPH TO THE ISHMEELITES FOR TWENTY PIECES OF SILVER: and they brought Joseph into Egypt.

Genesis 37:27-28

The salvation and deliverance of Joseph was paid for by silver. Silver speaks of the salvation of apparently insignificant souls! Joseph was a poor slave and prisoner! His salvation did not seem to matter to anyone. Silver was used to buy Joseph out of the pit. Through this one pitiful soul, an entire nation was saved.

Silver always speaks of salvation, deliverance and restoration. Silver is used in the building of God's residence. The salvation of apparently insignificant souls will always bring the presence of God. Jesus said, "I was hungry, I was thirsty, I was sick, I was naked, I was in prison and I was a stranger." These kinds of people are insignificant in society. No one cares about them. Yet Jesus cares about each and every single one of them. Do you care about insignificant souls? When you start caring about insignificant souls, you would have added silver to your ministry. The salvation of people is key to bringing the presence of God to your life and ministry.

Look at how Billy Graham started and ended. He preached about salvation from beginning to end. He was honoured by God to live a long and fruitful life. In his death, he was remembered by the whole world. All the living United States presidents honoured him in his death. Yet he never preached about politics, business, the marketplace or financial engineering. He preached about Jesus Christ and Him crucified. Is it not amazing that this simple, apparently irrelevant message of salvation and redemption brought him such acclaim?

Do not leave out the message of salvation and redemption! Salvation is still the most important message. Do not take any notice of these modern messages that set aside Jesus Christ and His message of salvation. Do not accept another gospel into your life! Do not accept the "money" gospel! Do not accept the good life and happiness gospel! Do not accept the business gospel! Stay with the Jesus gospel! Stay with salvation! Stay with redemption!

CHAPTER 12

Onyx Stones and God's Presence

And the Lord spake unto Moses, saying, Speak unto the children of Israel, that they bring me an offering: of every man that giveth it willingly with his heart ye shall take my offering.

And this is the offering which ye shall take of them; gold, and silver, and brass, And blue, and purple, and scarlet, and fine linen, and goats 'hair, And rams' skins dyed red, and badgers' skins, and shittim wood, Oil for the light, spices for anointing oil, and for sweet incense, ONYX STONES, and stones to be set in the ephod, and in the breastplate.

Exodus 25:1-7

And onyx stones, and stones to be set for the ephod, and for the breastplate... AND THE RULERS BROUGHT ONYX STONES, and stones to be set, for the ephod, and for the breastplate;

Exodus 35:9, 27

Onyx stones were precious stones used to create a meeting place for the presence of God.

Onyx stones are hard, black, unusual and valuable.

God loves to have unusual people who are solid as a rock. Nothing can move them! Nothing can break them! It is interesting that onyx stones were laid on the heart of the High Priest.

Do you mind being unusual? Do you mind being odd? Do you mind having odd people around you? It is the presence of all these different people that create the aura of God's presence. People who have only one type of person in their congregation do not experience the aura of God's presence. When the hands of many different people from different nations, different tribes and different tongues are lifted up to glorify God, there is a presence you cannot deny.

Onyx stones were also used in the ephod of the High Priest who came into the holiest of places. Onyx stones were used on the ephod and breastplate of the High Priest. The stones were set, solid and unmoveable. Indeed, the presence of God is magnificent and glorious. It is important to create a glorious environment if you want to experience the presence of God.

The use of onyx stones in the ephod of the priest is a revelation of how to create an environment for the presence of God. You must use onyx stones. Onyx stones signify the glorious presence of God. God will not inhabit the places that do not have onyx stones. With onyx stones, His presence will be multiplied in your ministry.

Onyx stones speak of something hard, something unyielding, something valuable and something outstanding. Indeed, when you are serving the Lord, you must be hard and unyielding in your determination to follow Him. You must be hard and determined to fulfil the call of God, no matter what and no matter who!

If you do not build the Tabernacle with onyx stones, you will not experience God's presence in the highest way.

The hardness of onyx stones speaks of those who will never change their minds about loving Him. You may change your mind about other things but do not change your mind about God. When such unusual onyx stones are part of the congregation, the presence of God is beautiful.

In the Scriptures, Onyx Stones lead to the glorious presence of God.

1. Onyx stones are fixed, unmovable stones.

> Now I have prepared with all my might for the house of my God the gold for things to be made of gold, and the silver for things of silver, and the brass for things of brass, the iron for things of iron, and wood for things of wood; ONYX STONES, AND STONES TO BE SET, glistering stones, and of divers colours, and all manner of precious stones, and marble stones in abundance.
>
> 1 Chronicles 29:2

Onyx stones speak of people that are set in your heart and in your life. The key characteristics of onyx stones are that they are set and unmoveable stones. There are people that God gives you for your ministry. They are set in your heart. They will never leave you. They are part of your life. They are set onyx stones. The presence of such people around you creates an aura of peace, stability and faithfulness. This aura is conducive to the presence of God.

The presence of faithful people is important to experience God's presence. The presence of wicked, disloyal and treacherous people brings about the presence of devils rather than the presence of God.

2. Onyx stones are precious and valuable stones.

> Thou hast been in Eden the garden of God; EVERY PRECIOUS STONE was thy covering, the sardius, topaz, and the diamond, the beryl, THE ONYX, and the jasper,

> the sapphire, the emerald, and the carbuncle, and gold: the workmanship of thy tabrets and of thy pipes was prepared in thee in the day that thou wast created.
>
> Ezekiel 28:13

Black unusual onyx stones are important, precious components of your ministry. They are precious stones. These unusual black stones are set on your heart and are so valuable for your ministry. Perhaps these onyx stones are more valuable than all the money you have in your ministry. People are more valuable than money. Good people are worth millions and millions of dollars. A faithful man, who can find? One person can be worth far more than any amount of money you could ever have.

Most people do not know the value of people so they mishandle them.

3. Onyx stones are foundation stones.

> THE FOUNDATIONS OF THE WALL OF THE CITY WERE ADORNED with every kind of jewel. The first was jasper, the second sapphire, the third agate, the fourth emerald, the fifth onyx, the sixth carnelian, the seventh chrysolite, the eighth beryl, the ninth topaz, the tenth chrysoprase, the eleventh jacinth, the twelfth amethyst.
>
> Revelation 21:19-20 (ESV)

The foundations of the city were made up of precious stones including the onyx stones. Onyx stones speak of the foundations of your ministry. You cannot build a great ministry with unfaithful people. The onyx stone speaks of something that is set and unmoveable. Something that is close to the heart.

When I started out in ministry, I had disloyal, murmuring people all around me. The ministry would not flourish and I could not advance at all. One day, I decided to cast out all the mockers of my life and ministry. Many people left the church. I was left with very few onyx stones that were set on my heart.

Years later, I realised that I had taken the right decision. Foundations are built with precious, fixed onyx stones and not rebellious and mobile jewels.

The foundation of your ministry must be with set onyx stones. That is how you will have the presence of God in your life and ministry. You will have the presence of God when you have a good foundation.

CHAPTER 13

Shittim Wood and God's Presence

And thou shalt make STAVES OF SHITTIM WOOD, and overlay them with gold.

Exodus 25: 13

And THOU SHALT MAKE BOARDS FOR THE TABERNACLE OF SHITTIM WOOD standing up. Ten cubits shall be the length of a board, and a cubit and a half shall be the breadth of one board.

Exodus 26: 15-16

And thou shalt make a vail of blue, and purple, and scarlet, and fine twined linen of cunning work: with cherubims shall it be made: And thou shalt hang it upon FOUR PILLARS OF SHITTIM WOOD overlaid with gold: their hooks shall be of gold, upon the four sockets of silver... And thou shalt make for the hanging FIVE PILLARS OF SHITTIM WOOD, and overlay them with gold, and their hooks shall be of gold: and thou shalt cast five sockets of brass for them.

Exodus 26:31-32, 37

Thou shalt also make A TABLE OF SHITTIM WOOD: two cubits shall be the length thereof, and a cubit the breadth thereof, and a cubit and a half the height thereof.

Exodus 25:23

And he made the altar of BURNT OFFERING OF SHITTIM WOOD: five cubits was the length thereof, and five cubits the breadth thereof; it was foursquare; and three cubits the height thereof.

Exodus 38:1

The use of shittim wood in the Tabernacle is a revelation of how to create God's residence. Shittim wood was used in the outer court whilst gold was used in the holy places. Shittim wood was used in the making of the joints of the tent. Shittim wood was also used for the boards of the Tabernacle, the poles of the wall, the pillars and the table of shewbread. Indeed, shittim wood was used to support the whole building.

Shittim wood was special because it did not decay easily. Shittim wood speaks of doing the work of God in such a way that it will not deteriorate or wither away quickly. I once attended a funeral in Europe. The coffin was remarkably simple and looked a little cheap. One of the family members explained to me. He said, "In this cemetery, we are not allowed to use quality wood. We are only allowed to use coffins made of cheap wood that decays, disintegrates and dissolves quickly." The cemetery wants the body and the wood of the coffin to dissolve as fast as possible because they need to give the space to another dead person. This cemetery would certainly not want coffins made out of shittim wood.

You must build the Tabernacle of God with shittim wood. Shittim wood signifies something that does not deteriorate or decay. God will not inhabit places that are not made out of shittim wood. God's presence will not be found in ministries that are decaying and failing.

Earthly things fade away quickly. Buildings fade away quickly. People fade away quickly! But the word of God endures forever! The churches that Apostle Paul built no longer exist. But the words that he wrote to Timothy are still being read today. Shittim wood speaks of being involved in long lasting ministry. Shittim wood speaks of ensuring that your ministry does not deteriorate and fade away quickly.

Shittim wood is resistant to decay and endures for a long time. You can practically invoke the presence of God by doing things that have eternal value rather than doing things that are short-lived. Many churches are short-lived. They last for a few years and are gone forever. Let us learn from our fathers who built churches that exist up till today.

If you do not build the Tabernacle according to His pattern, God will not inhabit it. God does not want you to do things that decay and deteriorate quickly. God's presence will not inhabit decaying things.

Build a church that will last forever. Build a church with young people who can take over the church when you are gone. Build a church that has many options for its leadership. Do not build a church that depends on one man. If you are that one great man, on whom everything depends, what will happen when you are gone? The presence of God is found in permanent things like shittim wood.

CHAPTER 4

Badgers' Skin and God's Presence

And thou shalt make a covering for the tent of rams 'skins dyed red, and A COVERING ABOVE OF BADGERS' SKINS.

Exodus 26:14

And the covering of rams 'skins dyed red, and THE COVERING OF BADGERS' SKINS, and the vail of the covering,

Exodus 39:34

"Badgers' skin" was the ugly skin of a badger that was used as a roof for the house of God. They did not have roofing tiles or roofing sheets in those days. Badgers' skin was ugly but nicely resisted the rain and elements.

You must build with badgers' skin if you want to have God's presence. God will not inhabit the places that do not follow His prescription. Without the element of badgers' skin, His presence will not be with you in your ministry.

What does badgers' skin speak of? Badgers' skin speaks of the physical covering over the presence of God. Badgers' skin was used in the covering of the Tabernacle.

The sturdy, resistant covering over the Tabernacle, speaks of the sturdy resistant covering that we need to enjoy God's presence. It is true that God's presence is found where two or three are gathered in His name. This may be under a tree or by the roadside. However, having your own building with your own roof over your head changes the level of your ministry. You will experience the presence of God when you are stable with a protective roof over your head. Churches that have buildings and roofs are more likely to experience God's presence. Build a church! Get a roof over your congregation! Enough with temporary structures! Enough with tents! You need the tough badgers' skin to protect the tabernacle (the presence of God).

The ugly badgers' skin also speaks of the faulty and failing human fathers and pastors whom God gives us to cover our heads in ministry. A man of God who has no covering will not experience the presence of God in his ministry.

Churches that are all alone, having no relationships, no covering or no fathers, lack something important. The presence of God is not felt or experienced in a certain way when there is no covering. It is important to be under a covering if you want to experience the presence of God. You can practically invoke the presence of God by being under God's covering.

I remember a dream that a pastor had. In the dream, he was preaching to a large crowd and I was standing behind him. Then I faded away. And as I faded away, the crowds began to disperse. It happened three times. Each time I faded away, the crowd dispersed. God spoke to him and told him that I was an important covering for his ministry. Every pastor who is a covering for you is human. He will have ugly faults no matter who he is.

Indeed, having a fault-ridden human pastor as a covering is the same as having the ugly, scarred and spotted badgers' skin as a covering for the Tabernacle.

If you do not do the ministry according to the pattern God gives, His presence will not be with your ministry. Like Moses, we need to go everywhere with the presence of God. "My presence shall go with thee, and I will give thee rest. And he said unto him, If thy presence go not with me, carry us not up hence" (Exodus 33:14-15). Do not be a loner! Be humble and relate with whoever God places over you. You will have the presence of God in your life and ministry.

CHAPTER 5

Goats' Hair and God's Presence

And thou shalt make CURTAINS OF GOATS' HAIR to be a covering upon the Tabernacle: eleven curtains shalt thou make.

Exodus 26:7

In Scripture, Goats' Hair Speaks of Human Sins

And he shall set the sheep on his right hand, but THE GOATS ON THE LEFT.

Matthew 25:33

Mine anger was kindled against the shepherds, and I PUNISHED THE GOATS: for the Lord of hosts hath visited his flock the house of Judah, and hath made them as his goodly horse in the battle.

Zechariah 10:3

And he shall take the two goats, and present them before the Lord at the door of the Tabernacle of the congregation. And Aaron shall cast lots upon the two

goats; one lot for the Lord, and the other lot for the scapegoat. And Aaron shall bring the goat upon which the Lord 's lot fell, and offer him for a sin offering. BUT THE GOAT, ON WHICH THE LOT FELL TO BE THE SCAPEGOAT, shall be presented alive before the Lord, to make an atonement with him, and to let him go for a scapegoat into the wilderness.

Leviticus 16:7-10

Different materials have symbolic meanings and we can learn these from the Bible. Goats' hair was used in the curtains of the Tabernacle. Goats' hair denotes the presence of a goat somewhere.

A goat always represents a sinner! Goats' hair represents the sinner. A goat represents that which is unacceptable! Goats' hair, therefore, represents that which is unacceptable. A goat represents that which must be punished! A goat represents failure! Goats' hair represents human failure that must be punished.

You must build with goats' hair. Goats' hair signifies the human failings and weaknesses that are ever present in men. God has decided to use failing and sinful human beings. He has decided to inhabit the place where failure-ridden human beings are. God is aware of our sins. As His presence is with us, it is with the knowledge of our many sins. He knows our weaknesses and they are before Him all the time.

A goat represents that which is unacceptable. Goats' hair represents traces of human sins that are always present when we go to the presence of God. It is important to acknowledge your sins if you want to experience the presence of God.

You can practically invoke the presence of God by acknowledging your human weaknesses. Jesus told a story of a man who went to the temple and acknowledged his sins. Another proclaimed his goodness, claiming he had fasted and paid tithes. But Jesus said the one who acknowledged his sin went away more righteous (Luke 18:10-14). Indeed, you may wonder what goats' hair is doing in the presence of God. The goats' hair is to remind you to acknowledge your sins.

If you do not acknowledge your sins, you will not experience the presence of God. The goats' hair that hangs in the presence of God is the continual acknowledging of human sins as we attempt to serve God. Following God is "the art of being a bad person who is trying hard to serve God".

A true spiritual leader must accept the presence of failures and spiritual weaklings. A true spiritual leader must acknowledge and welcome people who are laden with sins. Jesus said, "Come unto me all ye that labour and are heavy laden…" (Matthew 11:28). God wants to be in the midst of men. Men are dirty sinners, no matter how "good" they are. There will always be goats' hair in the presence of God!

God's presence can be with you even when you have sinned. When Jonah sinned and was in the belly of the whale, God remembered him. God's presence was with him in the belly of the whale and God helped him. God will help you. God's presence will be with you even in your sin and in your mistake.

CHAPTER 16

Rams' Skin Dyed Red and God's Presence

And THOU SHALT MAKE A COVERING FOR THE TENT OF RAMS' SKINS DYED RED, and a covering above of badgers' skins.

Exodus 26:14

Rams' skin was used in the building of the Tabernacle. Why did God want rams' skin? Did the rams' skin help to invoke the presence of God? Rams' skin has a symbolic meaning.

We can understand what a ram signifies by studying the word of God. The use of rams' skin in the Tabernacle is a revelation of how to build God's residence.

You must build with rams' skin. Rams' skin signifies consecration and sacrifice.

God will not inhabit the places that do not have the element of sacrifice and consecration. Rams' skin speaks of the great sacrifice that is required of all those who follow Jesus Christ. When a hall is filled with people who have sacrificed for Jesus Christ, there is a great and undeniable presence. Without rams' skin, His presence will not be with you in your ministry.

"Rams' skin dyed red" was used in the covering of the tent. Rams' skin dyed red speaks of the sacrifice that takes place to cover you.

1. "Rams' skin dyed red" speaks of Consecration to God.

And he brought the other ram, THE RAM OF CONSECRATION: and Aaron and his sons laid their hands upon the head of the ram.

Leviticus 8:22

It is important to be dedicated to God if you want to experience the presence of God. You can practically invoke the presence of God by being dedicated and consecrated to the service of God. In the presence of God, there is always consecration, sacrifice and dedication. Jesus spoke about how His father would never leave Him because He was dedicated and consecrated.

And he that sent me is with me: the Father hath not left me alone; FOR I DO ALWAYS THOSE THINGS THAT PLEASE HIM.

John 8:29

Dedication, sacrifice and consecration cause the Father to be pleased with you always!

2. "Rams' skins dyed red" speaks of Sacrifice.

And Abraham lifted up his eyes, and looked, and behold behind him A RAM CAUGHT IN A THICKET by his horns: and Abraham went and took the ram, and offered him up for a burnt offering in the stead of his son.

Genesis 22:13

Without sacrifice and consecration, your ministry will lack an important quality. Many people want to serve God without sacrifice. None of our Old Testament fathers served the Lord without sacrifice. I know many lay people who preach my messages as well as I do. However, many of them lack a certain quality because they are not prepared to give up anything for God. Abraham made sacrifices to God! Isaac made sacrifices to the Lord! Jacob made sacrifices to God! David made sacrifices to God! Solomon made sacrifices to God!

The ram that Abraham sacrificed was a ram of his consecration and dedication to God. It was the ram of his sacrifice.

CHAPTER 17

The Gate to His Presence

The hangings of one side of THE GATE shall be fifteen cubits: their pillars three, and their sockets three . . .

And for THE GATE of the court shall be an hanging of twenty cubits, of blue, and purple, and scarlet, and fine twined linen, wrought with needlework: and their pillars shall be four, and their sockets four.

Exodus 27:14, 16

And THE HANGING FOR THE GATE OF THE COURT WAS NEEDLEWORK, OF BLUE, AND PURPLE, AND SCARLET, AND FINE TWINED LINEN: and twenty cubits was the length, and the height in the breadth was five cubits, answerable to the hangings of the court. And their pillars were four, and their sockets of brass four; their hooks of silver, and the overlaying of their chapiters and their fillets of silver. And all the pins of the Tabernacle, and of the court round about, were of brass.

Exodus 38:18-20

There is a gate to your house. There is a gate to your residence. There is a gate to where you dwell. Indeed, there is a gate to God's house. There is a gate to God's residence. There is a gate to the presence of God! The gate to the presence of God in the Tabernacle was found in a small section of the white linen cloth. This section of the linen cloth was made out of colourful scarlet, purple and blue material. In other words, the colourful section of the white linen wall was the gate. This colourful cloth gate measured twenty cubits (thirty feet).

The gate to the Tabernacle was the entrance to the open-air compound. In that open-air compound was a tent which housed the Holy Place and the Holy of Holies. The actual presence of God was found in the Holy Place and the Holy of Holies.

Every single person, from the High Priest to the ordinary worshipper would have to enter through this single brightly coloured curtain that stood out from the white linen curtained wall.

Jesus Christ is the key to the presence of God. No one can come to the Father unless he comes through Jesus. If you magnify Jesus, you will experience the presence of God. If you set aside Jesus, you will not experience the presence of God. Today, there are ministries that exalt the wisdom and principles of business. Human ideas are magnified rather than the worship of Jesus Christ.

In such places you will not experience the presence of God. You experience the presence of God where Jesus Christ is lifted up. You must be careful to notice the absence of the presence of God. The presence of God is clearly absent in many churches. Many churches are simply lecture halls and motivation centres holding seminars and symposiums. The worship of Jesus Christ and the exaltation of the Son of God are missing in such places. Always remember, you cannot have the presence without the gate!

The Presence and the Gate

1. The gate speaks of the fact that there is only one way to heaven.

The gate of the court was the only way into the court just as Jesus Christ is the only way to the Father and to the presence today.

I am the gate; whoever enters through me will be saved. They will come in and go out, and find pasture.

John 10:9 (NIV)

2. The colours of the gate speak of Jesus Christ.

The Tabernacle gate was easy to find because it stood out. This speaks of how easy it is for anyone at all to find his way to God through Jesus Christ. You do not have to be very educated, very clever or very trained to notice the gate. Jesus is noticed by everyone. He is different from every other man. Jesus Christ stands out. Even those with the lowest understanding can find Jesus because He is the most unusual, amazing and colourful man that walked the earth over two thousand years ago.

3. All the colours of the Tabernacle contrasted sharply with the white tent and speak of Jesus Christ; who is a unique and unusual man.

The colours of the Tabernacle contrasted sharply with the tent just as Jesus contrasts sharply with other men. The gate is outstanding! Jesus is outstanding! Jesus' teaching is outstanding! Jesus' miracles are outstanding! The healings that Jesus performed are outstanding! Jesus' rising from the dead makes Him most outstanding! Jesus is remarkable, unusual and clearly distinguished from every other man.

4. **The blue colour in the gate speaks of Jesus Christ coming from the blue sky of heaven.**

5. **The white colour in the gate speaks of Jesus Christ who is holy and spotless.** Jesus Christ is the Lamb of God who was perfect.

6. **The purple colour in the gate speaks of the royalty of Jesus Christ. Jesus Christ is the King of kings.** When Jesus was tortured, the soldiers put on Him a purple robe.

And the soldiers platted a crown of thorns, and put it on his head, and they put on him a purple robe, . . . Then came Jesus forth, wearing the crown of thorns, and the purple robe. And Pilate saith unto them, Behold the man!

John 19:2, 5

7. **The scarlet colour in the gate speaks of the blood sacrifice that Jesus Christ made for the whole world.** His blood flowed from His head, His hands, His feet, His back and His side to save the world.

CHAPTER 18

The Door to His Presence

And thou shalt make an hanging for THE DOOR OF THE TENT, of blue, and purple, and scarlet, and fine twined linen, wrought with needlework. And thou shalt make for the hanging five pillars of shittim wood, and overlay them with gold, and their hooks shall be of gold: and thou shalt cast five sockets of brass for them.

Exodus 26:36-37

And he made an hanging for THE TABERNACLE DOOR of blue, and purple, and scarlet, and fine twined linen, of needlework; and the five pillars of it with their hooks: and he overlaid their chapiters and their fillets with gold: but their five sockets were of brass.

Exodus 36:37-38

There was a five-pillar door to the inner tent. This door was actually another colourful curtain hanging on five pillars. Going through this door would lead you straight to the Holy Place. What does this mean? Through Jesus, the gate, we come to the presence of God. But yet, there is another door through which we can go deeper. What does this second colourful curtain entrance represent?

I believe that the five pillars represent the five-fold ministry. Today,. it is the five-fold ministry that brings you near to God. Through apostles, prophets, pastors, teachers and evangelists, multitudes are brought close to God. He gave these gifts to men until we all come close to God. He gave these gifts to men until we all are so close to the Lord and are united with Him. He gave these gifts to men until we all become like Jesus.

> **And he gave some, apostles; and some, prophets; and some, evangelists; and some, pastors and teachers; For the perfecting of the saints, for the work of the ministry, for the edifying of the body of Christ: Till we all come in the unity of the faith, and of the knowledge of the Son of God, unto a perfect man, unto the measure of the stature of the fulness of Christ:**
>
> **Ephesians 4:11-13**

Over the years, I notice that people do not become close to God until they accept apostles, prophets, pastors, teachers and evangelists. They are doors for you! I have become closer to God by accepting great prophets like Kenneth Hagin into my life. I have become close to God by accepting great pastors like Yonggi Cho into my life. He was a door for me to get closer to God.

Those who are too stiff to accept to go through these doors will never experience a certain level of the presence of God. You cannot go far without true apostles and prophets. You will not get far without a pastor, a teacher or an evangelist. I would not be where I am today without wonderful teachers like Kenneth Hagin and Derek Prince. I would not be where I am today without wonderful evangelists like Reinhard Bonnke or Benny Hinn. Through such people, you can get closer to God.

Some people will say, "Do not trust a man." They will say, "Be careful of these money-grabbing men of God." What is actually happening is that you are being driven away from the five-pillared door to the presence of God. It is time to go through the five-pillared door into the Holy Place! It is time to receive your apostle, prophet and pastor so that you can be near to God. There is much more to the Lord than you are experiencing now. If you are not tired of learning, you will not be tired of rising into higher heights!

CHAPTER 19

The Veil to His Presence

And thou shalt make a vail of blue, and purple, and scarlet, and fine twined linen of cunning work: with cherubims shall it be made: And thou shalt hang it upon four pillars of shittim wood overlaid with gold: their hooks shall be of gold, upon the four sockets of silver.

And thou shalt hang up the vail under the taches, that thou mayest bring in thither within the vail the ark of the testimony: and the vail shall divide unto you between the holy place and the most holy.

And thou shalt put the mercy seat upon the ark of the testimony in the most holy place. And thou shalt set the table without the vail, and the candlestick over against the table on the side of the Tabernacle toward the south: and thou shalt put the table on the north side.

Exodus 26:31-35

The veil was the third entrance to the presence of God. In order to get to the deepest part of the Tabernacle, you would need to go through three colourful curtain doors. Each of these curtain entrances has a different name. The first curtain is called "the gate". The second curtain is called "the door" and the third curtain is called "the veil".

The "four-pillared curtain gate" speaks of Jesus who is the only way to God.

The five-pillared door speaks of the fivefold ministry, which is the way to know God even further. The veil speaks of the flesh of Jesus Christ that hid the glory of God from the eyes of man. When Jesus walked the earth, the glory of God was hidden from men. They thought He was a carpenter. They thought He was Joseph's son. They thought He had a normal family with brothers and sisters. They could not see the glory of God. The powerful glory of the eternal Son of God was completely hidden by the flesh of the human being. This glory of God was so concealed that human beings mobbed Jesus Christ and murdered the Son of God thinking that He was just an ordinary person.

1. Notice how the writer of Hebrews tells us that the veil is the flesh of Jesus Christ.

Having therefore, brethren, boldness to enter into the holiest by the blood of Jesus, by a new and living way, which he hath consecrated for us, THROUGH THE VEIL, THAT IS TO SAY, HIS FLESH;

Hebrews 10:19-20

2. Jesus Christ came into this world and gave His body to be broken and torn apart, like a veil, for the salvation of this world.

And when he had given thanks, he brake it, and said, Take, eat: THIS IS MY BODY, WHICH IS BROKEN FOR YOU: this do in remembrance of me.

1 Corinthians 11:24

3. When Jesus' body was broken, the veil in the temple was also torn apart. The tearing away of the veil symbolized the removal of the thing that had hidden God from man. The veil that covered God had now been torn apart and God was available to man.

Jesus, when he had cried again with a loud voice, yielded up the ghost. And, behold, THE VEIL OF THE TEMPLE WAS RENT IN TWAIN from the top to the bottom; and the earth did quake, and the rocks rent; And the graves were opened; and many bodies of the saints which slept arose, And came out of the graves after his resurrection, and went into the holy city, and appeared unto many.

Matthew 27:50-53

4. The flesh of Jesus Christ is important for you to experience the presence of God. Every time you have communion, you eat the flesh of Jesus Christ and tear away the veil to the presence of God.

For my flesh is meat indeed, and my blood is drink indeed. He that eateth my flesh, and drinketh my blood, dwelleth in me, and I in him.

John 6:55-56

People who have communion and believe in it deeply experience a greater presence of God. The flesh of Jesus Christ is the veil and that veil is torn away in communion, revealing the presence of God. He that eats the flesh and drinks the blood experiences the dwelling of the presence of God.

There is a church that has emphasized the Holy Communion for hundreds of years. Even though hundreds of years have gone by, they still represent God and Jesus Christ in a way that many churches do not.

It is the constant tearing of the veil that has allowed the presence of God to continue in that church, making it one of the most prominent and powerful churches in the world today.

After the same manner also he took the cup, when he had supped, saying, This cup is the new testament in my blood: this do ye, as oft as ye drink it, in remembrance of me. For as often as ye eat this bread, and drink this cup, ye do shew the Lord's death till he come.

1 Corinthians 11:25-26

CHAPTER 20

The Altar of Sacrifice and the Presence

AND THOU SHALT MAKE AN ALTAR OF SHITTIM WOOD, five cubits long, and five cubits broad; the altar shall be foursquare: and the height thereof shall be three cubits.

Exodus 27:1

PLACE THE ALTAR OF BURNT OFFERING IN FRONT OF THE ENTRANCE TO THE TABERNACLE, the Tent of Meeting;

Exodus 40:6 (NIV)

The altar of sacrifice was the first item to see in the compound of God's residence. Without making a sacrifice on the altar, there was no way to proceed further and deeper into the presence of God.

There is no way to serve God without sacrifice. Everyone who came close to God paid the price and made a sacrifice. If you want to experience the presence of God, you must pay the price and make the sacrifice God requires of you. All through the scripture, the presence of God was manifested where people made sacrifices.

There are people who preach the same thing as others. But you never sense the presence of God in a certain way. The reason is simple - there is no sacrifice behind the preaching. There is no altar of sacrifice hidden from view. The man of God has not been to the altar of sacrifice. Yes, he is a preacher but there is no presence. Yes, he preached a sermon but there was no presence. I dare you to watch Christian television and listen to Christian preachers. You will notice that many good ideas and theories are expounded but not all have the presence of God in their ministries. We need the altar of sacrifice. We need to pay the price. We need to give up our own ambitions and lay them on the altar. We need to give up certain friendships and lay them on the altar. If need be, we need to sacrifice our fathers, mothers, brethren, sisters, wives, children and even our own lives also.

If any man come to me, and hate not his father, and mother, and wife, and children, and brethren, and sisters, yea, and his own life also, he cannot be my disciple.

Luke 14:26

Please take note of the fact that all who ever served God and enjoyed His presence, had to serve Him with a sacrifice.

1. Aaron offered sacrifices to God and saw the presence of God.

> And the breasts and the right shoulder Aaron waved for a wave offering before the Lord; as Moses commanded. And Aaron lifted up his hand toward the people, and blessed them, and came down from offering of the sin offering, and the burnt offering, and peace offerings.
>
> And Moses and Aaron went into the Tabernacle of the congregation, and came out, and blessed the people: and THE GLORY OF THE LORD APPEARED unto all the people. And there came a fire out from before the Lord, and consumed upon the altar the burnt offering and the fat: which when all the people saw, they shouted, and fell on their faces.
>
> Leviticus 9:21-24

2. David offered many sacrifices to God and saw the presence of God.

He made great sacrifices for the Ark of God. The Ark of God represented the presence of God. In order for the Ark of God to move closer, he had to make some sacrifices.

> And it was told king David, saying, The Lord hath blessed the house of Obed-edom, and all that pertaineth unto him, because of the ark of God. So David went and brought up the ark of God from the house of Obed-edom into the city of David with gladness. And it was so, that WHEN THEY THAT BARE THE ARK OF THE LORD HAD GONE SIX PACES, HE SACRIFICED OXEN AND FATLINGS.
>
> 2 Samuel 6:12-13

This story shows us how King David made innumerable sacrifices as he brought in the Ark of God. The Ark of God represents the presence of God. After every six steps, they would sacrifice oxen and fatling. Can you imagine how many sacrifices they must have made from Obed-edom's house to the City of David? This journey of David symbolizes how sacrifice brings in the presence of God. It is time to believe in His presence. Expect the presence as you serve the Lord. Expect the presence of God on earth. Give yourself to Him. The presence of God is worth your sacrifice!

3. Solomon offered sacrifices to God and saw the presence of God.

> Also king Solomon, and all the congregation of Israel that were assembled unto him before the ark, SACRIFICED SHEEP AND OXEN, WHICH COULD NOT BE TOLD NOR NUMBERED FOR MULTITUDE…. It came even to pass, as the trumpeters and singers were as one, to make one sound to be heard in praising and thanking the Lord; and when they lifted up their voice with the trumpets and cymbals and instruments of musick, and praised the Lord, saying, For he is good; for his mercy endureth for ever: that THEN THE HOUSE WAS FILLED WITH A CLOUD, EVEN THE HOUSE OF THE LORD; So that the priests could not stand to minister by reason of the cloud: for THE GLORY OF THE LORD HAD FILLED THE HOUSE OF GOD.
>
> 2 Chronicles 5:6, 13-14

As you can see in this account, when the Israelites offered sacrifice, the presence of God came down. Do you want to see the presence of God in your life? Then do not shy away from the sacrifice that God has placed before you. A minister who has the presence of God on his life has paid the price.

In this account, Solomon sacrificed thousands of bullocks. Solomon made many sacrifices to the Lord. Suddenly, the presence of God filled the temple and no one could stand to minister. God was apparently moved by the sacrifice. God is still moved by your sacrifice! The presence of God will appear when you make a good sacrifice!

CHAPTER 21

The Laver and the Presence

And the Lord spake unto Moses, saying, thou shalt also make A LAVER OF BRASS, and his foot also of brass, to wash withal: and thou shalt put it between the Tabernacle of the congregation and the altar, and thou shalt put water therein. For AARON AND HIS SONS SHALL WASH THEIR HANDS AND THEIR FEET THEREAT: When they go into the Tabernacle of the congregation, they shall wash with water, that they die not; or when they come near to the altar to minister, to burn offering made by fire unto the Lord: So they shall wash their hands and their feet, that they die not: and it shall be a statute for ever to them, even to him and to his seed throughout their generations.

Exodus 30:17-21

And he made the LAVER OF BRASS, and the foot of it of brass, OF THE LOOKINGGLASSES OF THE WOMEN assembling, which assembled at the door of the Tabernacle of the congregation.

Exodus 38:8

The laver of brass was a metal bowl filled with water. You would have to wash your hands after handling the blood on the altar of sacrifice. This is a clear step in the journey to the presence of God - the laver filled with water for the washing of your hands and feet. The laver was actually built with the mirrors of the women. This meant that you could see your reflection in the water as you washed your hands. This container of water was a prophetic foretelling of the importance of the word of God. Without the cleansing of your mind, your mind will never be able to experience the presence of God in a certain way.

1. The laver of brass speaks of self-assessment through the Word.

> **For if any be a hearer of the word, and not a doer, he is like unto a man beholding HIS NATURAL FACE IN A GLASS: For he beholdeth himself, and goeth his way, and straightway forgetteth what manner of man he was.**
>
> **James 1:23-24**

The laver was built with the mirrors of the women and so you could see a reflection of yourself as you washed your hands. Clearly, the laver was a prophetic description of something that you can use to assess yourself.

The laver, therefore, prophetically speaks of the Word of God. In order to experience the presence of God, you need the word of God. All through the Bible, the washing with water speaks of the word of God cleansing you. Jesus said, "You are clean through the word which I have spoken unto you."

You are cleansed by the washing of the water of the Word! The doctrines of the Word of God are described as rain!

2. The laver of brass speaks of cleansing through the Word.

> **Now ye are CLEAN THROUGH THE WORD which I have spoken unto you.**
>
> **John 15:3**

> **Give ear, O ye heavens, and I will speak; and hear, O earth, the words of my mouth.**
>
> **Deuteronomy 32:1**

> **That he might sanctify and cleanse it with the WASHING OF WATER BY THE WORD, That he might present it to himself a glorious church, not having spot, or wrinkle, or any such thing; but that it should be holy and without blemish.**
>
> **Ephesians 5:26-27**

The laver of brass is for the cleansing and renewing of your mind. Without a renewed mind you cannot go far with God.

The Word of God is key to experiencing the presence of God. You cannot have your church service without the Word of God. The Word of God sets the tone and gives the direction for all that we are supposed to do. God is His Word! God is in His Word!

There are some ministers who behave as though the preaching of the Word is contrary to the power and the presence of God. They say things like, "I will be finished with this preaching very soon and we can get into the prophetic and the power." It is as though the preaching of the Word hinders the presence of God. On the contrary, the presence of God is encouraged by the word of God. We are nothing without the word of God. We know God through His word. We must hold on to the Word and embrace it fully. It is the master key to the presence of God.

Indeed, just before you enter the Holy Place, you need to deal with the laver which has the water of the Word. That shows how close the laver is to the Holy of Holies and the presence of God.

3. The laver of brass speaks of growth through the Word.

MY DOCTRINE SHALL DROP AS THE RAIN, my speech shall distil as the dew, as the small rain upon the tender herb, and as the showers upon the grass:

Deuteronomy 32:2

The rain brings growth! The word of God brings growth! Wherever the word of God is, there is growth, there is increase and there is plenty. As the word of God increased, the number of disciples multiplied. Multiplication will take place in your ministry when the word of God is increased. Never think that the word of God is contrary to the presence and power of God.

And the word of God increased; and the number of the disciples multiplied in Jerusalem greatly; and a great company of the priests were obedient to the faith.

Acts 6:7

CHAPTER 22

The Shewbread and the Presence

Thou shalt also make a table of shittim wood: two cubits shall be the length thereof, and a cubit the breadth thereof, and a cubit and a half the height thereof. And thou shalt overlay it with pure gold, and make thereto a crown of gold round about. And thou shalt make unto it a border of an hand breadth round about, and thou shalt make a golden crown to the border thereof round about. And thou shalt make for it four rings of gold, and put the rings in the four corners that are on the four feet thereof. Over against the border shall the rings be for places of the staves to bear the table. And thou shalt make the staves of shittim wood, and overlay them with gold, that the table may be borne with them. And thou shalt make the dishes thereof, and spoons thereof, and covers thereof, and bowls thereof, to cover withal: of pure gold shalt thou make them. And THOU SHALT SET UPON THE TABLE SHEWBREAD BEFORE ME ALWAY.

Exodus 25:23-30

Moses placed the table in the Tent of Meeting on the north side of the Tabernacle outside the curtain and SET OUT THE BREAD ON IT before the Lord, as the Lord commanded him.

Exodus 40:22-23 (NIV)

The shewbread is the bread that the priests ate when they went into the Holy Place. Bread represents the word of God and the shewbread represents the word of God meant for pastors and ministers. Many of Kenneth Hagin's messages were directed at ministers of the gospel. It was when I started feeding on his messages that I experienced the presence of God.

Many television ministers and authors are preaching good messages. These messages are good for ordinary Christians. However, many of these ministers and authors are not giving shewbread to priests. There is a difference between simple Christian messages, which are intended to encourage baby Christians, and shewbread messages that are good for ministers of the gospel.

Indeed, there are messages from the word of God that are meant only for those in ministry. Every minister who wants to experience the power and the presence of God must eat shewbread. Not all pastors can minister to other pastors. Not all of them have the gift of relating with and teaching other ministers. Shewbread represents the messages from the word of God that are specifically for those in ministry.

> **And he said unto them, have ye never read what David did, when he had need, and was an hungred, he, and they that were with him? How he went into the house of God in the days of Abiathar the high priest, and DID EAT THE SHEWBREAD, WHICH IS NOT LAWFUL TO EAT BUT FOR THE PRIESTS, and gave also to them which were with him?**
>
> **Mark 2:25-26**

Even in the Bible, you will notice that some letters are addressed to pastors. The books of Timothy and Titus are shewbread because they are addressed to ministers of the gospel. These letters are shewbread. Paul wrote to Timothy and asked him to be a good minister. Paul wrote to Titus and asked him to stay behind and set things in order. These were not messages to the congregation. These were messages to the pastors. These were shewbread messages!

> **If thou put the brethren in remembrance of these things, THOU SHALT BE A GOOD MINISTER OF JESUS CHRIST, nourished up in the words of faith and of good doctrine, whereunto thou hast attained.**
>
> **1 Timothy 4:6**

> **For this cause LEFT I THEE IN CRETE, THAT THOU SHOULDEST SET IN ORDER THE THINGS that are wanting, and ordain elders in every city, as I had appointed thee:**
>
> **Titus 1:5**

People do not develop in the ministry because they listen to messages meant for ordinary Christians. You must expose yourself to messages that are for meant for ministers. Dear man of God, there are higher messages intended for you. Dear man of God, there are deeper things meant just for you. The more you eat the shewbread, the more you will experience God's presence!

CHAPTER 23

The Candlestick and the Presence

And thou shalt make A CANDLESTICK OF PURE GOLD: of beaten work shall the candlestick be made: his shaft, and his branches, his bowls, his knops, and his flowers, shall be of the same. And six branches shall come out of the sides of it; three branches of the candlestick out of the one side, and three branches of the candlestick out of the other side: Three bowls made like unto almonds, with a knop and a flower in one branch; and three bowls made like almonds in the other branch, with a knop and a flower: so in the six branches that come out of the candlestick. And in the candlestick shall be four bowls made like unto almonds, with their knops and their flowers.

Exodus 25:31-34

The candlestick was the only source of light in the Holy Place. Remember that the Holy Place was a tent without windows. There were no inlets of light at all in the Holy Place. The candlestick contained the oil that burned and provided light in the Holy Place. The candlestick clearly represents the Holy Spirit's direction and guidance for your life and ministry.

As you get closer to the presence of God, you cannot depend on "natural light" at all. You must depend more and more on supernatural guidance for everything that you do. You cannot claim to have wisdom if you do not know what the will of God is.

Through the supernatural guidance of the Spirit, you will know the appointed times of God. You will accomplish great things for God because His wisdom will be deep in you. It is only when you follow the supernatural light of God that you come into His presence.

All animals have a supernatural guiding force within them. They are able to migrate hundreds of miles without a compass of any sort. These animals have never been to school.

> **Yea, the stork in the heaven knoweth her appointed times; and the turtle and the crane and the swallow observe the time of their coming; but my people know not the judgment of the Lord. HOW DO YE SAY, WE ARE WISE, and the law of the Lord is with us? Lo, certainly in vain made he it; the pen of the scribes is in vain. The wise men are ashamed, they are dismayed and taken: lo, they have rejected the word of the Lord; and what wisdom is in them?**
>
> **Jeremiah 8:7-9**

Animals have no technology at their disposal but they know where to go and how to go to places. This is supernatural! God's word teaches us that if we cannot match the animals in supernatural guidance, we are not yet wise. Through the Holy Spirit you will have supernatural guidance and be able to match the animals in their supernatural knowledge and timings. From today, you will know supernatural timings and judgments. As you increase in your ability to be guided supernaturally, you will get nearer the presence of God.

> And the angel that talked with me came again, and waked me, as a man that is wakened out of his sleep, And said unto me, What seest thou? And I said, I have looked, and behold A CANDLESTICK ALL OF GOLD, WITH A BOWL UPON THE TOP OF IT, AND HIS SEVEN LAMPS THEREON, and seven pipes to the seven lamps, which are upon the top thereof: And two olive trees by it, one upon the right side of the bowl, and the other upon the left side thereof. So I answered and spake to the angel that talked with me, saying, What are these, my lord? Then the angel that talked with me answered and said unto me, Knowest thou not what these be? And I said, No, my lord. Then he answered and spake unto me, saying, This is the word of the Lord unto Zerubbabel, saying, Not by might, nor by power, but by my spirit, saith the Lord of hosts.
>
> Zechariah 4:1-6

Zechariah saw in the visions of God the golden candlestick, its seven lamps and seven pipes. The candlestick was being fed with olive oil by olive trees on the side. He asked the angel what it meant and the angel explained that it was a vision of the Holy Spirit.

Zechariah's vision of the candlestick was a vision of the Holy Spirit's guidance. It was a vision of how the building of the temple would be accomplished without human strength and without human abilities but with the mighty Spirit of God.

The candlestick always represents the supernatural guidance of the Spirit of God. Supernatural guidance of the Holy Spirit makes you powerful. Supernatural guidance of the Holy Spirit makes you a builder. Supernatural guidance of the Holy Spirit makes you accomplish great things for God. Supernatural guidance of the Holy Spirit enables you to finish the temple of God and experience the presence of God.

CHAPTER 24

The Altar of Incense and the Presence

And THOU SHALT MAKE AN ALTAR TO BURN INCENSE UPON: of shittim wood shalt thou make it. A cubit shall be the length thereof, and a cubit the breadth thereof; foursquare shall it be: and two cubits shall be the height thereof: the horns thereof shall be of the same. And thou shalt overlay it with pure gold, the top thereof, and the sides thereof round about, and the horns thereof; and thou shalt make unto it a crown of gold round about.

Exodus 30:1-3

And THOU SHALT MAKE AN ALTAR TO BURN INCENSE UPON: of shittim wood shalt thou make it. A cubit shall be the length thereof, and a cubit the breadth thereof; foursquare shall it be: and two cubits shall be the height thereof: the horns thereof shall be of the same. And THOU SHALT OVERLAY IT WITH PURE GOLD, the top thereof, and the sides thereof round about, and the horns thereof; and thou shalt make unto it a crown of gold round about.

Exodus 30:1-3

AARON MUST BURN FRAGRANT INCENSE ON THE ALTAR every morning when he tends the lamps. he must burn incense again when he lights the lamps at twilight so that incense will burn regularly before the Lord for the generations to come.

Exodus 30:7-8 (NIV)

Moses placed the gold altar in the tent of meeting in front of the curtain AND BURNED FRAGRANT INCENSE ON IT, as the Lord commanded him.

Exodus 40:26-27 (NIV)

The altar of incense was a master key to entering the presence of God. Obviously, the incense from the Holy Place would filter in from the Holy of Holies where the ultimate presence of God dwelt.

1. Incense speaks of your prayers that bring the presence of God.

> LET MY PRAYER BE SET FORTH BEFORE THEE AS INCENSE; and the lifting up of my hands as the evening sacrifice.
>
> Psalms 141:2

> And another angel came and stood at the altar, having a golden censer; and there was given unto him much incense, that he should offer it with the prayers of all saints upon the golden altar which was before the throne. And THE SMOKE OF THE INCENSE, WHICH CAME WITH THE PRAYERS of the saints, ascended up before God out of the angel's hand.
>
> Revelation 8:3-4

> And when he had taken the book, the four beasts and four and twenty elders fell down before the Lamb, having every one of them harps, and GOLDEN VIALS FULL OF ODOURS, WHICH ARE THE PRAYERS OF SAINTS.
>
> Revelation 5:8

This is an important revelation. We have, in the scripture, glimpses of heaven. These glimpses of heaven have shown us that our prayers ascend as incense before God. God receives our prayers and offerings as incense that is filtering upwards. Incense creates an atmosphere that is both seen and smelt by the one who is in it. God both sees and smells your prayers and this draws you into the presence of God. All through the scripture, incense has been set forth as a type of prayer. Prayer definitely brings in the presence of God.

2. Incense speaks of your offerings that bring the presence of God.

> And when they were come into the house, they saw the young child with Mary his mother, and fell down, and worshipped him: and when they had opened their treasures, they presented unto him gifts; gold, and frankincense, and myrrh.
>
> Matthew 2:11

Incense is more than prayer! It is your prayer and your offerings! When Jesus was born, wise men came from the east with three gifts: myrrh, gold and frankincense. Frankincense is white incense! Frankincense is the highest type of pure incense. Frankincense was presented as a special gift to Jesus. Frankincense, therefore, was a type of offering presented to the Lord. Offerings can bring in the presence of God and change the course of events in your life.

Your powerful offering can ascend as a type of prayer that can change God's mind. For instance, the king of Moab and the Moabites were condemned to defeat and destruction. The prophet had prophesied their destruction and they were doomed.

> But now bring me a minstrel. And it came to pass, when the minstrel played, that the hand of the Lord came upon him. And he said, Thus saith the Lord, Make this valley full of ditches. FOR THUS SAITH THE LORD, Ye shall not see wind, neither shall ye see rain; yet that valley shall be filled with water, that ye may drink, both ye, and your cattle, and your beasts. AND THIS IS BUT A LIGHT THING IN THE SIGHT OF THE LORD: HE WILL DELIVER THE MOABITES ALSO INTO YOUR HAND. AND YE SHALL SMITE EVERY FENCED CITY, AND EVERY CHOICE CITY, and shall fell every good tree, and stop all wells of water, and mar every good piece of land with stones.
>
> 2 Kings 3:15-19

This prophecy spelt doom for the Moabites. We know that God is not a man that He should lie (Numbers 23:19). We know that when Elisha spoke the word of God it was sure and the Moabites were doomed. There was no way the Moabites were going to escape. However, the king changed the course of the prophecy by his offering. The offering that he gave released such power that the word of God was altered and the destruction intended for Moab was diverted.

> And when the king of Moab saw that the battle was too sore for him, he took with him seven hundred men that drew swords, to break through even unto the king of Edom: but they could not.
>
> THEN HE TOOK HIS ELDEST SON THAT SHOULD HAVE REIGNED IN HIS STEAD, AND OFFERED HIM FOR A BURNT OFFERING UPON THE WALL. And there was great indignation against Israel: and they departed from him, and returned to their own land.
>
> 2 Kings 3:26-27

You can divert all doom and destruction that is headed towards you by your offerings. You can bring down the presence of God by the sweet-smelling prayers and the amazing offerings that you have for the Lord.

CHAPTER 25

The Holy of Holies

And thou shalt hang up the vail under the taches, that thou mayest bring in thither within the vail the ark of the testimony: and the vail shall divide unto you between the holy place and THE MOST HOLY. And thou shalt put the mercy seat upon the ark of the testimony in the most holy place. And thou shalt set the table without the vail, and the candlestick over against the table on the side of the Tabernacle toward the south: and thou shalt put the table on the north side.

Exodus 26:33-35

The ultimate presence of God was found in the Holy of Holies. The Holy of Holies had the mercy seat, the cherubims, the Ark of the Covenant and the tables of testimony: The High Priest who entered into the Holy of Holies encountered these four major items; the mercy seat, the cherubims, the Ark of the Covenant and the tables of testimony.

1. **The ark of God covered with gold speaks of the high price for God's presence.**

> And THEY SHALL MAKE AN ARK OF SHITTIM WOOD: two cubits and a half shall be the length thereof, and a cubit and a half the breadth thereof, and a cubit and a half the height thereof. And THOU SHALT OVERLAY IT WITH PURE GOLD, within and without shalt thou overlay it, and shalt make upon it a crown of gold round about . . . And thou shalt put into the ark the testimony which I shall give thee.
>
> Exodus 25:10-11, 16

The ark of God represents the ultimate presence of God. The ultimate presence of God is not easy to define. It is dangerous to walk in sin or play the fool in the presence of God. The ark is completely covered with gold. Only the highest quality and the most expensive can have access to the ultimate presence of God. Brass is not acceptable if you want to experience the ultimate presence of God.

Many people have a ministry that outwardly looks shiny and valuable. However, they have substituted real value and have presented only an outward glitter. God looks at the heart. God looks at the realities. It is important for you to focus on real things because God is not impressed with outward-looking niceties. Indeed, people may not be impressed with you but Almighty God may be impressed because you have used gold for the ministry and paid a high price to get it.

2. The tables of testimony speak of the higher purposes of God.

> **And thou shalt put the mercy seat above upon the ark; and IN THE ARK THOU SHALT PUT THE TESTIMONY THAT I SHALL GIVE THEE.**
>
> **Exodus 25:21**

Within the ark you will find the tables of testimony. These tables contain the ultimate purposes of God. When you go near the presence of God, you understand His purposes.

The Ten Commandments are a set of instructions from God. Everybody knows these Ten Commandments. But what is God's purpose in revealing these Ten Commandments? When you are far from the presence of God, you may know His commandments but not understand His purposes.

God has purposed many things but few people know what God has purposed. It takes closeness to God to understand His purposes! When you are close to God, you will understand what He is trying to do. You are confused because you do not understand the purposes of God. Why did God let this person live? Why did God let this person die? Why does God allow certain things to happen?

> **This is the purpose that is purposed upon the whole earth: and this is the hand that is stretched out upon all the nations. For the Lord of hosts hath purposed, and who shall disannul it? and his hand is stretched out, and who shall turn it back?**
>
> **Isaiah 14:26-27**

3. The cherubims represent the ever present angels in the presence of God.

> **And make TWO CHERUBIM OUT OF HAMMERED GOLD AT THE ENDS OF THE COVER. Make one cherub on one end and the second cherub on the other;**

make the cherubim of one piece with the cover, at the two ends. THE CHERUBIM ARE TO HAVE THEIR WINGS SPREAD UPWARDS, overshadowing the cover with them. The cherubim are to face each other, looking towards the cover.

Exodus 25:18-20 (NIV)

There are always angels in the presence of God. God is never without angels. Every revelation of God's presence reveals multitudes of angels. When you experience the presence of God, you will experience what it is like to be in the presence of many angels. The presence of God is characterized by the presence of angels. It is a bit like having ants around sugar. They just come around because of the sugar.

Angels are always there when God is there. Anyone who sees a lot of angels is seeing the presence of God. Be grateful when anyone spots angels around you. It is a sign of God's presence. You may see the angels but you may not see God. But the presence of the angels is a sure sign that God is nearby.

He that overcometh, the same shall be clothed in white raiment; and I will not blot out his name out of the book of life, but I will confess his name before my Father, and BEFORE HIS ANGELS.

Revelation 3:5

And I beheld, and I heard the voice of MANY ANGELS ROUND ABOUT THE THRONE and the beasts and the elders: and the number of them was ten thousand times ten thousand, and thousands of thousands;

Revelation 5:11

4. The Mercy Seat speaks of God's mercy and grace.

And THOU SHALT MAKE A MERCY SEAT of pure gold: two cubits and a half shall be the length thereof, and a cubit and a half the breadth thereof.

Exodus 25:17

The mercy seat is the place where you receive the mercies of God. The Bible teaches us to come boldly to the throne of grace so that we can receive mercy and grace to help in time of need.

> **Let us therefore come boldly unto the throne of grace, that we may obtain mercy, and find grace to help in time of need.**
>
> **Hebrews 4:16**

There is really nothing much you can expect from the presence of God, other than mercy. By the time you arrive in His presence, you will be extremely conscious of your sin and shortcomings. Indeed, we are laden with sin and we are helplessly evil! Jesus said to His disciples whom He was training to be apos-tles, "If ye then, being evil, know how to give good gifts unto your children: how much more shall your heavenly Father give the Holy Spirit …" (Luke 11:13).

In this amazing scripture, Jesus called His disciples "evil men". His disciples had asked Him to teach them how to pray. He looked pitifully at them and said, "Even you evil people give good gifts; how much more My Father." Jesus knows how evil we are. Even disciples who want to learn about prayer are evil men. How much more those who are not disciples? How much more those who do not want to learn about prayer? Our condition is truly desperate! We need mercy and grace! We are basically evil! Are you not glad that there is a mercy seat in His presence? You will receive mercy when you seek to be close to God and when you seek to be in His presence.

CHAPTER 26

Going West Takes You Deeper

Deep calleth unto deep at the noise of thy waterspouts: all thy waves and thy billows are gone over me.

Psalms 42:7

Which direction are you facing? Are you facing the world and heading deeper into business, moneymaking and secular acclaim? Why are you so happy to be described as someone who appeals to the world as well as to the church? Why does worldly acclaim appeal to you? Instead of being a prophet of God, you are a secular mouthpiece, quoting the words of famous worldly men everywhere you go. Why are you happier to be associated with businessmen than with God's servants? This is happening because, spiritually speaking, you are completely oriented towards the east!

It is time for you to go deeper into the presence of God! You can go deeper! You have to orient yourself towards the presence of God. You have to orient your whole life towards following God and going deeper. Prophetically, this means you have to orient yourself towards the west. Going to the west means you are going deeper into the presence of God. Most Christians are oriented towards the east. Most Christians are oriented towards earthly things. Earthly things have left you dry! Earthly things will always leave you dry!

Many ministers are not eternity-minded. They are oriented towards earthly things. Worldly goals have filled the hearts of God's servants. Evil ambitions of being business tycoons have captured the hearts of God's humble servants. Your evil desires draw you towards the east. Adam, Eve, Cain and Lot all went east! Their hearts were oriented in a direction that took them away from God. Instead of becoming shallower, worldlier, more earthly and more carnal, you must become deeper, more spiritual and more heavenly-minded. The desire for earthly things has left the church dry, parched and barren. How come much of the church is oriented towards the east?

1. **The deepest innermost back part of the Tabernacle was towards the west. When you walk deeper into the presence of God, you would be walking west.**

This meant that when you were going deeper into the Tabernacle you were going westwards. The Holy of Holies was deep inside the Tabernacle towards the west. Going deeper into the presence of God means you are going towards the west.

> And make the boards for the Tabernacle [in the following quantities]: twenty boards for the south side; And you shall make forty silver sockets under the twenty boards, two sockets under each board for its two tenons. And for the north side of the Tabernacle there shall be twenty boards. And their forty silver sockets, two sockets under each board. For THE BACK OR WEST SIDE of the Tabernacle you shall make six boards.
>
> Exodus 26:18-22 (AMPC)

2. **The front of the Tabernacle faced east. When you walk away from the Tabernacle and the presence of God, you would be walking east.**

This meant that when you were going out of the Tabernacle you would be going eastwards. This also meant that when you were going away from the presence of God, you would be going towards the east.

> And likewise for its length on the north side there shall be hangings a hundred cubits long, its pillars twenty and their bases twenty, of bronze, but the hooks of the pillars and their fillets shall be of silver. And for the breadth of the court on the west side there shall be hangings for fifty cubits, with ten pillars and ten bases. The breadth of the court on THE FRONT TO THE EAST shall be fifty cubits.
>
> Exodus 27:11-13 (ESV)

3. **The gates of all Jewish temples and places of worship face the east. When you walk away from the temple and away from the presence of God, you would be walking east.**

> The man brought me back to the entrance of the temple, and I saw water coming out from under the threshold of

> the TEMPLE TOWARD THE EAST (FOR THE TEMPLE FACED EAST). The water was coming down from under the south side of the temple, south of the altar. He then brought me out through the north gate and led me around the OUTSIDE TO THE OUTER GATE FACING EAST, and the water was flowing from the south side.
>
> Ezekiel 47:1-2 (NIV-MIT)

Coming into the temple and going deeper into the temple meant that you were going west. *Going west always speaks of going towards God whilst going east always speaks of going away from God.* Going west symbolizes moving deeper into God.

The Holy of Holies, (the deepest part of the Tabernacle) was on the west end of the courtyard. Going west symbolized moving toward God. Going east symbolized going away from God.

The Holy of Holies, the dwelling place of God in the Tabernacle, was on the west end of the courtyard.

All through the Bible, going east has meant going away from God. Going west has meant going deeper into God.

God is not everywhere in the same way. God will give you the direction in which you must go. As you can see, going east is going away from God's presence. It is important that you follow the direction of the Holy Spirit. You must orient yourself towards where God's presence is. God is not everywhere in the same way. God is place-sensitive. God is sensitive to direction. You cannot just point yourself in any direction. You must be oriented towards God!

In Deuteronomy 12:13-14, the scripture teaches that God chooses where He wants people to worship Him. God says, "I don't want you to worship me just anywhere." From today, God will choose your direction and your orientation. God may orient you towards a man of God, towards a ministry or towards a church. Accept the orientation that He gives you and flow in that direction.

God is not flowing everywhere in the same way. Go west into the presence of God. Go deeper into the Tabernacle by going west. Go deeper into God's residence by going deeper into the prophetic and mystical western horizon of your life. Do not try to be like the world! Do not try to have as many degrees as your worldly counterparts! Do not try to have as much money as your worldly counterparts! Do not try to be worldly!

4. **Adam and Eve went east when they were driven away from the presence of God! Going east symbolizes going away from God. The gate of the Garden of Eden was on the east side.**

And the Lord God said, Behold, the man is become as one of us, to know good and evil: and now, lest he put forth his hand, and take also of the tree of life, and eat, and live for ever: Therefore the Lord God sent him forth from the garden of Eden, to till the ground from whence he was taken. SO HE DROVE OUT THE MAN; AND HE PLACED AT THE EAST OF THE GARDEN OF EDEN CHERUBIMS, and a flaming sword which turned every way, to keep the way of the tree of life.

Genesis 3:22-24

5. **Cain went east! Cain went away from the presence of God to the land of Nod, east of Eden.**

And the Lord said unto him, therefore whosoever slayeth Cain, vengeance shall be taken on him sevenfold. And the Lord set a mark upon Cain, lest any finding him should kill him. And CAIN WENT OUT FROM THE PRESENCE OF THE LORD, AND DWELT IN THE LAND OF NOD, ON THE EAST OF EDEN.

Genesis 4:15-16

6. **Lot went east! Lot split from Abraham, went east, and landed in the evil cities of Sodom and Gomorrah.**

Is not the whole land before thee? Separate thyself, I pray thee, from me: if thou wilt take the left hand, then I will go to the right; or if thou depart to the right hand, then I will go to the left. And Lot lifted up his eyes, and beheld all the plain of Jordan, that it was well watered every where, before the Lord destroyed Sodom and Gomorrah, even as the garden of the Lord, like the land of Egypt, as thou comest unto Zoar. Then Lot chose him all the plain of Jordan; AND LOT JOURNEYED EAST: and they separated themselves the one from the other. Abram dwelled in the land of Canaan, and Lot dwelled in the cities of the plain, and pitched his tent toward Sodom.

Genesis 13:9-12

7. **Rebellious people who serve idols face the east because they are oriented away from God.**

And he brought me into the inner court of the Lord 's house, and, behold, at the door of the temple of the Lord, between the porch and the altar, were about five and twenty men, WITH THEIR BACKS TOWARD THE TEMPLE OF THE LORD, AND THEIR FACES TOWARD THE EAST; and they worshipped the sun toward the east.

Ezekiel 8:16

References

Chapter 8

Sapphire Stones Retrieved from: http://www.ggapcpakistan.com/Sapphire.html. April 2019

Chapter 26

Overview of Tabernacle Gate of the Court, Jack Zavada Retrieved from:https://www.thoughtco.com/tabernacle-gate-of-the-court-700103. April 2019